TEACH YOUR
DOG
CRAZY
TRICKS

13-Digit ISBN: 978-1-64643-183-0
10-Digit ISBN: 1-64643-183-9

This book may be ordered by mail from the publisher. Please include $5.99 for postage and handling.

Please support your local bookseller first!

Books published by Cider Mill Press Book Publishers are available at special discounts for bulk purchases in the United States by corporations, institutions, and other organizations. For more information, please contact the publisher.

Cider Mill Press Book Publishers
"Where good books are ready for press"
501 Nelson Place
Nashville, Tennessee 37214

cidermillpress.com

Typography: Gibson, Justus Pro
Image credits: patterns are used under official license from Shutterstock.com.
All other images courtesy of Cider Mill Press Book Publishers.

Printed in Malaysia

23 24 25 26 27 TJM 5 4 3 2 1
First Edition

TEACH YOUR DOG CRAZY TRICKS

50

Howl-arious Stunts,
from Walking Backward
to Fetching a Beverage

Desiree van Zon

Illustrated by Maggie Sullivan

CIDER MILL
PRESS

BOOK
PUBLISHERS

CONTENTS

INTRODUCTION

Hi! My name is Desiree van Zon, and I live in the Netherlands with my two border collies, Tess and Jill, whom I have been teaching tricks since they were pups.

I grew up on a farm and have been an animal lover all my life—goats, cows, horses, chickens, cats, dogs, rabbits, hamsters, you name it! Horses and ponies were a particular passion—training and riding them were two of my favorite activities. For a number of years I was involved in competitive riding but then became more interested in how to teach horses different tricks, like taking a bow and lying down on command.

Honestly, I didn't like dogs at all that much at first. On our farm, our dogs were less pets and more working dogs—mainly used for guarding. I knew dogs were being used for hunting, herding, retrieving, guiding, whatever was needed, but having a dog as a "pet" kind of seemed pointless until I was in my teens and I learned about dog sports, including teaching dogs tricks.

Around this time, my parents were looking for a new companion dog and researching breeds. When I learned about border collies, I was in love. Their energy, their unending will to please, incredible intelligence, and beauty really spoke to me. And I was utterly captivated by the videos I was watching of border collies performing tricks and competing in agility championships. It wasn't long after this that our first border collie joined the family—Tess.

She quickly became my furry best friend, and we became (and still are) inseparable. When she came home, we immediately started with basic puppy training and obedience classes. I watched videos online to learn how to teach Tess tricks. Once Tess was a year old, we started agility classes, at first just for fun, but soon we went to competitions where Tess performed amazingly well. She was also astounding at tricks, learning over 200 in the space of just a couple

of years. Before I knew it, we were being invited to model for photo shoots and give demonstrations at local events.

But besides sports, one of my favorite things to do with Tess is to travel. She has visited more than ten countries in Europe, with that number increasing nearly every year. Because of Tess, I took up photography and videography, as I wanted to capture all of our wonderful moments together in the best way possible. Soon I was sharing my photos and videos on YouTube and Instagram and through that connecting with many wonderful dog trainers all over the world.

In 2018, Tess injured her knee while playing Frisbee, which was the end of her agility career. Around this same time, I decided to enter a dog dance show. Unbelievably, Tess and I ended up winning the event! I got invited to become a member of the national dog dance bond and even got offered dog dance classes by one of the coaches, which, of course, I accepted. Thus began our dog dance career!

Dog dance is actually a lot harder than you might think. During a routine, the dog and human must move together as one, with

tricks, gestures, and movements blending smoothly into one another. Judges also want the dog and handler to tell a story with each dance, which requires a lot of creativity as well as training. The music, moves, clothes, and accessories must work together seamlessly.

There are two types of dog dance: heelwork to music and canine freestyle. Heelwork is closer in nature to obedience training, with the dog performing close to the human. In freestyle, it is preferred that the dog and handler work at some distance from each other and with much more creativity in regard to the moves (as long as they are safe for the dog to perform).

Tess and I soon were entering canine freestyle dance competitions, and, within four years, we reached the highest level in the Netherlands. In 2022, we became the Dutch champions in canine freestyle and competed in Freestyle Heelwork to Music at Crufts dog show in Birmingham, England, in 2023.

But Tess is aging—eleven at the writing of this book—which means that soon she'll have to retire from dog sports altogether. The thought of this greatly saddens me, as she is and will always be

the best dog I could have ever wished for. When we are working and training, I feel sometimes like she can read my mind.

About a year ago, we got a new addition to our family, a border collie puppy named Jill. She has a personality that is very different from Tess's—way more energetic, confident, and vocal, yet very sensitive. She is challenging me all over again when it comes to dog training.

One thing hasn't changed, though: the methods I use for teaching tricks. But in having to start again with a new pup, I've realized it can be hard to remember how exactly I taught Tess certain tricks initially. So I have written this book for myself but also for you, to make training a new dog a lot easier.

Desiree van Zon

Tess & Jill

TRICK TRAINING BASICS

Learning tricks should be a fun experience for both you and your dog. It is important to understand that the training involved in mastering the tricks in this book should be in an addition to basic obedience training. Before you start with even the easiest of the tricks included, your dog needs to understand and respond consistently to the voice commands fundamental to training: sit, lie down, stand, and stay. These commands are components in most of the tricks in this book.

TRAINING THE RIGHT WAY

I do not support punishment-based training. My method is to reward your dog when they show the desired behavior and to ignore your dog when they make a mistake or don't show the behavior you were aiming for.

Rewarding your dog can be done by giving treats or letting them play with a toy they like. It also helps to react enthusiastically when the dog shows the desired behavior. Each dog has their own preferences; experiment and go with what works best for your dog. Always make sure you have enough treats with you when training.

HEALTH AND AVOIDING INJURIES

Make sure your dog is in good physical health before starting training. There are some tricks in this book (they are all flagged) that are not recommended for dogs with obesity or joint issues (like elbow or hip dysplasia, osteoarthritis, etc.) or other physical disabilities that can affect their mobility. Some tricks will not be possible or recommended because of a dog's particular build (for instance, large or giant dogs, and in other cases, toy dogs) or a specific feature, like short paws or a snub nose. The same goes for puppies and young dogs; some tricks are not appropriate for them because it puts stress on still-developing bones, muscles, and tissues.

If you are in doubt as to whether or not your dog can or should perform a certain trick, we recommend that you consult with your veterinarian. Teaching your dog a trick should never compromise their health; the health of the dog should always be your number one priority!

You also need to be very careful not to overstress your dog during training. Balancing on an object or staying in a certain position, even if for just a few seconds, can ask a lot from your dog physically. It is easy to overwork your dog, and this is to be avoided. Pay attention to important but sometimes subtle signals from your pup, like shaking, a curved back (especially while standing), frequently lying down, excessive panting, lowered interest, failing tricks that went well before, and excessive barking and yawning, as these are all signs of fatigue. If your dog exhibits any of these, stop training immediately and be more mindful in future training sessions. You should never work your dog to the point that they start exhibiting these behaviors. By watching your dog closely, injuries can be avoided.

IT'S NOT A RACE

Some dogs learn faster than others, and some may never learn certain tricks. This may depend on the dog's temperament, their level of training, or just simply how well the dog understands what you are asking of them. This is okay! Some tricks will only take a few days for your dog to learn, while others can take several years. Small steps are the key. Follow your dog's pace and don't rush training. Rushing and/or putting pressure on the dog will only lead to stress, which will make it harder for your dog to learn and enjoy the training.

When starting to teach a new trick, do it in a calm, quiet environment the dog is used to, so the surroundings won't distract them. This will make it easier for the dog to pay attention to you. Once the dog understands what behavior you expect from them, you can move the training to another location that provides more distractions.

KNOWING WHEN TO STOP

Some dogs may get overstimulated quickly, which can lead to the dog becoming hyper; conversely, a dog can lose interest, simply shutting down and/or walking away, a signal to you that your dog is done with this training session. You want to avoid both situations, so keep each training session short, no longer than 15 minutes. It is best to have multiple short training sessions per day instead of a long one once every day or two.

It's also important to stop a training session while the dog is feeling positive. When your dog finally does that one thing you have been trying to teach them for a while, don't ask them to do it a second time. Instead, reward your dog as enthusiastically as you can with treats, a favorite toy, and/or lots of praise and stop the training. Ending the training this way will stimulate your dog to think about what they did that was so good they got rewarded so well for it, so they can do it again next time!

If your dog isn't understanding what you want, stop training that trick, ask the dog to do something you know that they do know how to do, reward for that, and try again later.

CLICKER TRAINING

A great little device to help you with training is a clicker. A clicker gives a clear and constant sound that helps mark the desired behavior. Unlike the tone of your voice or the words we use to mark

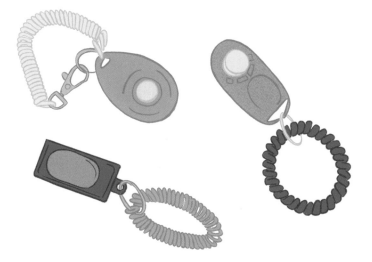

desired behaviors, a clicker always sounds the same. This makes it much easier for the dog to understand when exactly they showed the correct behavior, which then makes it easier for the dog to repeat this behavior for a reward. A click should always be immediately followed up by a reward, so that the dog knows that the click means a reward. This will encourage the dog to show the desired behavior.

Before using the clicker for training, the dog must learn that the click sound equals a reward. This is called "charging the clicker." It is best to use a treat as a reward for clicker charging. Make sure it is something your dog really likes!

1. Move yourself and your dog to a quiet room with no distractions. Hold the clicker in one hand and treats, in the other. Make sure you bring a treat pouch or bucket with treats and keep this close to you so there is quick access.

2. Press the clicker and immediately give or throw the dog a treat. This is called "click and treat."

3. Repeat this frequently for 2 to 5 minutes. Make sure every time you click and give a treat, the dog is doing something different from the last time you clicked (without you giving a command). This way you prevent the dog from associating the click and treat with any particular action. The one and only purpose of this training is to establish the link between the click and the treat.

4. Repeat this session regularly for a few days, until you are confident the dog understands the link. Once the clicker is "charged," it can be used to start teaching new tricks.

With clicker training, it is important to click at the exact moment the dog shows the desired behavior. If you click too early, you will reward the dog for starting a certain behavior but not performing the behavior itself; when you click too late, you are rewarding the dog for stopping the behavior.

VOICE COMMANDS

Besides or instead of the clicker, you can also introduce a verbal marker (for example, "yes!"). Verbal markers may not always work as well as a clicker, as we also use, for example, the word "yes" in our daily language, which may confuse the dog. But it is a great solution for when you want to mark a certain behavior and don't have the clicker at hand. You can get your dog used to voice commands the same way you would for a clicker (page 12).

In the step-by-step instructions for the individual tricks, I will describe marking a behavior through the use of a clicker and/or verbal markers. It is up to you what you prefer to use.

BEGINNER DOG TRICKS

These tricks are generally easy to teach and a good first step in trick training a dog. All of these tricks are easy to perform for most dogs.

GIVE PAW

This is one of the easiest tricks for your dog to learn.

COMMANDS/TRICKS YOUR DOG SHOULD KNOW

- Sit

WHAT YOU NEED

- Treats
- Clicker

TAKE IT UP A NOTCH: This trick is the basis of many others, like Wave Goodbye (page 20), Cross Paws (pages 154 and 158), and "Limp" on Command (page 196). To be able to teach those tricks, your dog needs to learn the difference between their left and right front paws. For the dog's right paw, you could use the command "paw," and for their left paw, "other one." Switch up which paw you ask for, so the dog learns the difference between the two.

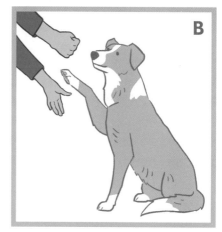

HOW TO TRAIN

1. Have the dog sit in front of you. It is easiest if you sit down as well.

2. Hold a treat in your hand and show this to the dog. **(Refer to example A.)**

3. Close your hand so the dog can't reach the treat. Sometimes dogs naturally offer their paw in an attempt to get to the treat in your hand.

   If your dog doesn't try to paw at your hand, hold the treat in one hand in front of the dog's nose and touch behind one front paw with your other hand. This should result in the dog lifting up their paw. **(Refer to example B.)**

4. When your dog lifts up a paw, say your command (for example, "paw") immediately, click, and then give the reward.

5. Repeat this several times, until you are confident the dog understands the behavior.

6. Now, instead of saying the command when the dog shows the behavior, use the command right before the dog shows the behavior, so they learn to give a paw when you ask for it.

7. Repeat this training several times, until your dog gives a paw every time you give the command.

WAVE GOODBYE

When your dog knows how to politely greet people by giving a paw, it is also fun to teach them to say goodbye!

COMMANDS/TRICKS YOUR DOG SHOULD KNOW

- Sit
- Give Paw (page 18)

WHAT YOU NEED

- Treats
- Clicker

A

B

HOW TO TRAIN

1. Have the dog sit in front of you.

2. Ask your dog to give a paw, but hold your hand a little higher and farther away from the dog, so they have to stretch their paw. When your dog lifts their paw up higher and farther than they would to give a paw, click and reward. **(Refer to example A.)**

3. Move your hand up a bit higher in each training session, until the dog is raising their paw above their head. **(Refer to example B.)**

4. Once the dog does this consistently, you can start adding a command (for example, "wave") each time the dog lifts up their paw.

5. Repeat this several times, until you are confident the dog understands the behavior. You can now start saying the command right before the dog shows the behavior. Reward when the dog waves after the command. If the dog doesn't respond to the command well, take a step back and try again later.

SPIN AROUND

Teaching your dog to spin is easy and makes for a great first dog dance move!

NOT SUITABLE FOR

- Dogs with osteoarthritis or other joint issues where sharp twists are discouraged.

COMMANDS/TRICKS YOUR DOG SHOULD KNOW

- Stand

WHAT YOU NEED

- Treats or a toy
- Clicker

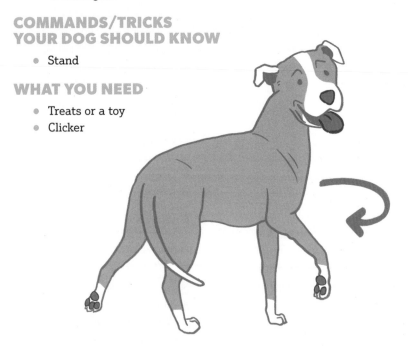

TAKE IT UP A NOTCH: Want to dance with your dog? Once your dog knows this trick, spin around yourself while your dog does a spin. If your dog spins counterclockwise, you spin clockwise, and vice versa. At first this might be confusing for your dog, but with some encouragement, most dogs will quickly understand what you expect from them. Reward your dog well when they twist together with you!

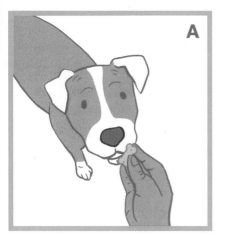

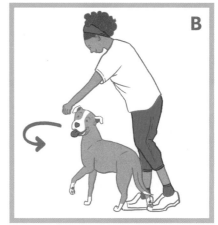

HOW TO TRAIN

1. Have the dog stand in front of you.

2. Hold a reward in your hand and keep it in front of the dog's nose. **(Refer to example A.)**

3. Move the hand with the treat in a circular movement around the dog. Move slowly at first, so the dog can easily follow your hand. Give praise and reward when the dog has made a full circle.

If your dog doesn't follow your hand fully, click and reward for each step your dog does take. If they understand this, then slowly move to rewarding for two steps, then three steps, etc.,until they make a full circle. **(Refer to example B.)**

4. Repeat this several times, until the dog consistently follows your hand in a full circle.

5. Now add a voice command every time your dog is about to spin around. You can use different commands for clockwise and counterclockwise turns (for example, "turn" and "twist").

6. During each training, try to reduce your hand signal by moving your hand away from the dog. When the dog knows to turn around with the use of the verbal command and either a minimal hand cue or none at all, your dog has mastered the trick!

WALK AROUND A PERSON/OBJECT

Have your dog walk around you or any random object. A useful trick for when the leash gets tangled around you!

WHAT YOU NEED

- Treats or a toy
- Clicker

TEACH YOUR DOG CRAZY TRICKS

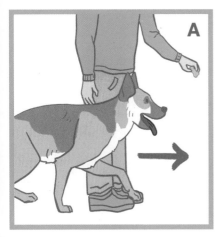

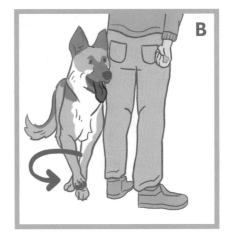

HOW TO TRAIN

WALK AROUND A PERSON

1. Put a reward in your hand, hold your hand in front of your dog's nose, and slowly move it away from your dog. When your dog follows, click, reward, and praise them. **(Refer to example A.)**

2. Lead your dog in a circle around you while you stand still. When doing this, switch the reward between your hands behind your back to make the circle. Reward your dog frequently to encourage them to keep following your hand. **(Refer to example B.)**

3. After a few training sessions, reduce the number of rewards you give and encourage your dog to make a complete circle in one go. Your goal is to give the dog a single reward after making a full circle around you.

CONTINUED...

4. Once the dog understands this, you can introduce a voice command (for example, "circle me" or "go round"; you can use different commands for clockwise and counterclockwise circles). Slowly reduce the hand luring by moving your hand away from the dog's nose and reducing the circular motion you make with your hand.

5. Once your dog masters this trick, they should walk around you in the requested direction after you give them the voice command. **(Refer to example C.)**

WALK AROUND AN OBJECT

1. To teach your dog to walk around another object (for example, a tree or a cone), the same steps should be followed, but instead you lure the dog around the object. **(Refer to example D.)**

TEACH YOUR DOG CRAZY TRICKS

LEG WEAVE

Have your dog weave between your legs when you stand still or walk.

NOT SUITABLE FOR

- Dogs with (severe) osteoarthritis or other joint issues.

COMMANDS/TRICKS YOUR DOG SHOULD KNOW

- Stand

WHAT YOU NEED

- Treats or a toy

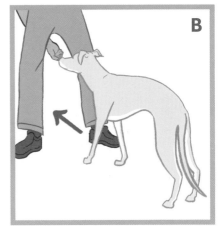

HOW TO TRAIN

1. Have the dog stand in front of you. **(Refer to example A.)**

2. Hold a reward in your right hand and hold this hand behind you, so that your dog can see it between your legs. Make sure there is enough space between your legs for your dog to walk through.

3. Lure your dog between your legs and reward them. **(Refer to example B.)**

CONTINUED...

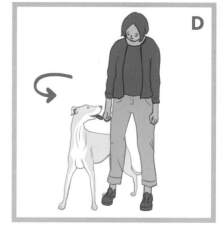

4. Lure the dog around you counterclockwise (with the reward in your right hand) until the dog stands in front of you again. Reward the dog. (**Refer to example C.**)

5. Repeat steps 2, 3, and 4, but with the reward in your left hand and luring the dog back clockwise.

6. Repeat these steps again, each time switching hands and steering your dog from your left side through your legs to your right side and back to create a weaving motion. (**Refer to example D.**)

7. Once your dog starts to understand the task, you can skip the reward right after they walk between your legs and immediately lure the dog to your front. There you will reward the dog.

TEACH YOUR DOG CRAZY TRICKS

PLAY DEAD (LYING ON SIDE)

This the most realistic version of "playing dead," with your dog lying down on their side.

COMMANDS/TRICKS YOUR DOG SHOULD KNOW

- Lie down

WHAT YOU NEED

- Treats
- Clicker

TEACH YOUR DOG CRAZY TRICKS

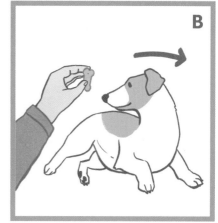

HOW TO TRAIN

1. Have the dog lie down in front of you. Sit or kneel so you are close to the dog. **(Refer to example A.)**

2. Hold a treat in your left hand and position it to the right side of the dog's head, close to their nose. Click and reward when the dog follows your hand.

3. Now move your hand toward the dog's shoulder. This will cause the dog to lean on their left side. Click and reward when the dog follows your hand. **(Refer to example B.)**

CONTINUED...

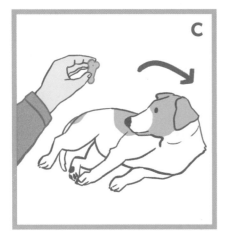

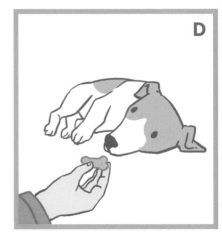

4. Repeat step 3 a few times, then move your hand closer to the dog's back until they have to fully lie on their side in order to reach your hand. Click, reward, and praise your dog well for lying down on their side. **(Refer to example C.)**

5. Once your dog is comfortable with lying down on their side, they have to learn to lay their head flat on the ground. With the dog lying on their side, move your hand directly to the ground in front of the dog. Hold the treat on the ground, between your fingers, so the dog has to touch the ground with their head to get to the treat. Click and reward when the dog touches the ground with their head while staying flat on their side. **(Refer to example D.)**

PLAY DEAD!

6. Repeat step 5 several times, until the dog understands they only get a treat when they stay flat on the ground and touch the ground with their head and nose.

7. Add a voice command (for example, "play dead" or "flat") each time your dog shows the desired behavior. In each training session, wait a little longer before you give the treat, so the dog learns that they have to hold the position to get rewarded.

8. When your dog masters this trick, they should be able to lie flat on their side on voice command.

PLAY DEAD (LEGS IN THE AIR)

This trick is not only cute, it's also very useful. With your dog on their back, it is easier to search them for ticks, treat the paws, and brush the belly.

COMMANDS/TRICKS YOUR DOG SHOULD KNOW

- Lie down
- Play Dead (Lying on Side) (page 32)

WHAT YOU NEED

- Treats
- Clicker

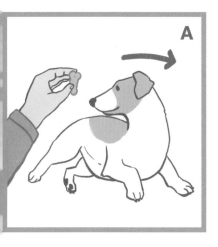

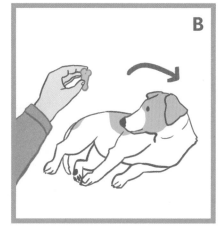

HOW TO TRAIN

1. Have the dog lie down in front of you. Sit or kneel so you are close to the dog.

2. Hold a treat in your left hand and position it to the right of your dog's head, close to their nose. Click and reward when the dog follows your hand. **(Refer to example A.)**

3. Now move your hand toward the dog's shoulder. This will cause the dog to lean on their left side. Click and reward when the dog follows your hand. **(Refer to example B.)**

CONTINUED...

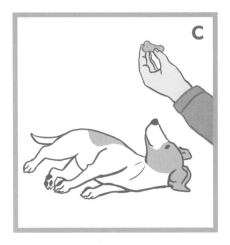

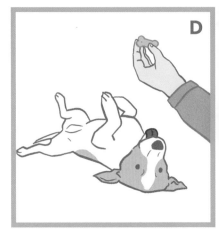

4. Repeat step 3 a few times, then move your hand closer to the dog's back until they have to fully lie on their side in order to reach your hand. Click, reward, and praise your dog well for lying down on their side. Continue to move your hand over the dog's back to their left side. When the dog is about to roll over, move your hand back to the dog's nose so the dog doesn't roll over completely. Immediately click and reward when the dog is positioned on their back. **(Refer to example C.)**

5. Repeat step 4 several times, and each time wait a bit longer before you click and reward, so the dog holds the position. **(Refer to example D.)**

6. When your dog understands the desired behavior, add a voice command (for example, "play dead" or "on your back"—make sure you use a different command from the lying on your side version of play dead) each time your dog rolls onto their back. When your dog masters this, they should be able to roll onto their back on command.

7. To get your dog to hold this position until you say otherwise, teach your dog a release command (for example, "free" or "okay"). When the dog has held the position long enough, reward them in that position, then say the release command enthusiastically and immediately lure your dog out of the position with a treat or toy. Reward the dog again. Repeat this several times, until your dog holds the position and only moves out of it on the release command.

ROLL OVER

A trick that never gets old. The training for it is similar to Play Dead (Legs in the Air), except the dog will do a full rollover.

COMMANDS/TRICKS YOUR DOG SHOULD KNOW

- Lie down

WHAT YOU NEED

- Treats
- Clicker

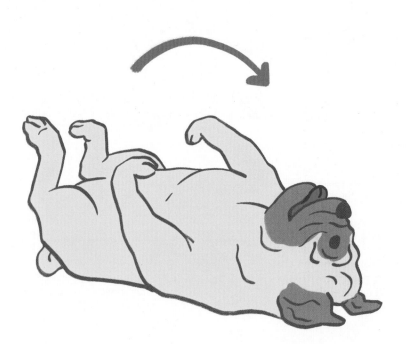

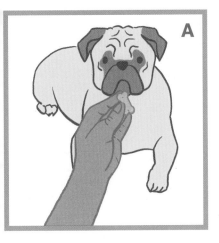

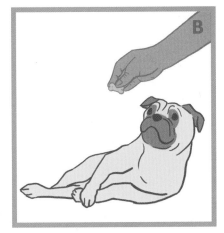

HOW TO TRAIN

1. Have the dog lie down in front of you. Sit or kneel so you are close to the dog.

2. Hold a treat in your left hand and position your hand to the right of the dog's head, close to their nose. Click and reward when the dog follows your hand. **(Refer to example A.)**

3. Now move your hand toward the dog's shoulder. This will cause them to lean on their left side. Click and reward when the dog follows your hand. **(Refer to example B.)**

4. Repeat step 3 a few times, and click and reward every time your dog moves their nose toward your hand.

CONTINUED...

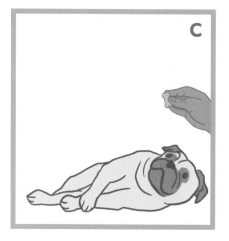

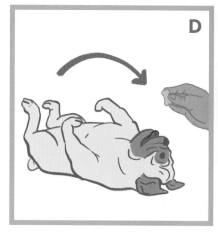

5. Now move your hand closer to the dog's back, until the dog has to fully lie on their side in order to reach your hand. **(Refer to example C.)**

6. Continue to move your hand over the dog's back to their left side. At this point, the dog can no longer reach your hand with their nose without rolling over. When the dog rolls over, click and reward immediately and praise the dog enthusiastically. **(Refer to example D.)**

7. Repeat step 6 several times, each time rewarding and praising the dog.

TEACH YOUR DOG CRAZY TRICKS

ROLL OVER!

8. Add a voice command (for example, "roll over") each time the dog rolls over.

9. When you are confident the dog understands the behavior, you can start to reduce the hand luring by slowly moving your hand away from the dog. When your dog masters this trick, they should be able to roll over on voice command with minimal or no hand luring.

WALK BACKWARD

Have your dog walk away from you backward. It's not only fun, it can come in handy—for example, when your dog stands in your way in front of a door.

COMMANDS/TRICKS YOUR DOG SHOULD KNOW

- Stand

WHAT YOU NEED

- A toy
- Clicker

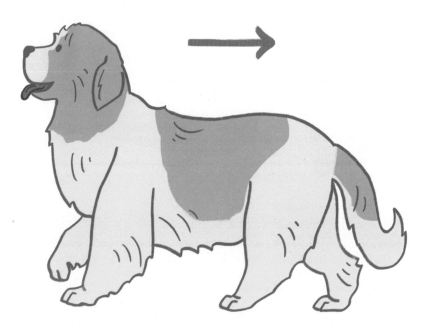

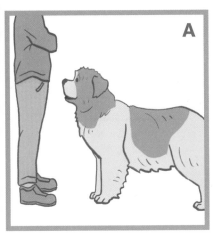

HOW TO TRAIN

1. Have the dog stand close in front of you. (**Refer to example A.**)

2. Start by taking a few (small) steps toward your dog. Most dogs will naturally take a few steps backward when you do this. If your dog doesn't, try leaning forward as you move toward your dog. (**Refer to example B.**)

3. When the dog takes a few steps backward, click and reward. When rewarding, either throw the reward or walk toward your dog to give the treat, so the dog doesn't step forward.

4. Repeat step 3, and click and reward every time your dog walks backward (make sure you only click when the dog is walking backward and not when the dog is already standing still).

5. When your dog consistently walks backward, add a voice command (for example, "go back" or "back up") each time the dog starts to take a step backward.

CONTINUED...

6. Now don't walk toward your dog at all; instead, just say the voice command. Click and reward immediately if the dog steps backward. It is likely the dog will take fewer steps backward when you start doing this, so it is important that you reward the dog immediately. **(Refer to example C.)**

7. When you are confident the dog understands the voice command, you can start adding distance. Wait a little bit longer before you reward your dog, so they take one extra step backward. If necessary, repeat the command for walking backward. Click and reward immediately when the dog takes an extra step backward.

8. Repeat step 7 and try to add more distance every few training sessions. Ideally, you don't want to have to repeat the command several times to have the dog walk back farther. To encourage your dog to keep walking backward, you can introduce a "stop" command. When your dog stands still, immediately say "stop" and reward. **(Refer to example D.)**

9. Switch between rewarding for walking backward and "stop," until the dog fully masters both.

CRAWL

Teaching your dog to do an army crawl is easy and looks very cool.

COMMANDS/TRICKS YOUR DOG SHOULD KNOW

- Lie down

WHAT YOU NEED

- Treats
- Clicker

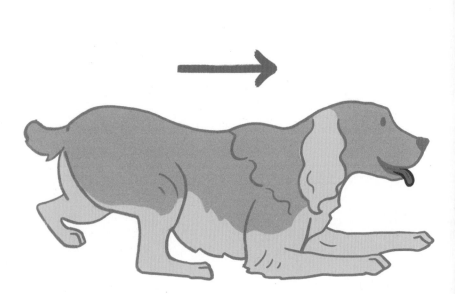

HOW TO TRAIN

1. Have your dog lie down in front of you as you stand. **(Refer to example A.)**

2. Lean forward and hold a treat in front of your dog's nose. Make sure you hold the treat low to the ground, so the dog is less likely to stand up. Slowly move the treat away from the dog's nose, so the dog will have to crawl to get to the treat. **(Refer to example B.)**

3. When the dog crawls forward, click and reward immediately (even if it is only one step).

There is a chance your dog will stand up to walk toward your hand. If this happens, walk the dog back to where they were lying down and try again. Soon the dog will realize that standing up will not get them the treat.

4. Repeat steps 2 and 3 several times, until you are confident the dog understands what is expected.

5. Add a voice command (for example, "crawl") each time your dog crawls.

CONTINUED...

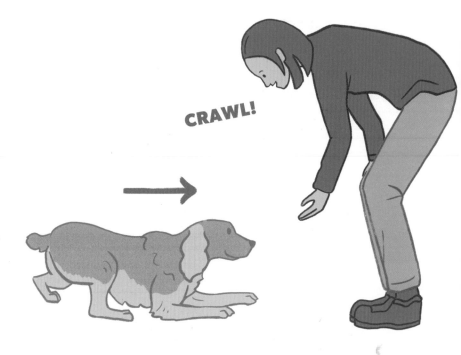

6. Once the dog responds well to the voice command, slowly start to put more distance between you and your dog. Instead of holding the treat directly in front of the dog's nose and luring from there, take half a step back so you create a small space between you and your dog. Now show your dog the treat and give the command to crawl. When the dog crawls, click, reward, and praise the dog well. Increase the distance a little bit with each training session, until the desired distance is achieved.

HEAD DOWN

This is probably one of the cutest photo poses for dogs!

COMMANDS/TRICKS YOUR DOG SHOULD KNOW

- Lie down
- Stay is helpful

WHAT YOU NEED

- Treats
- Clicker

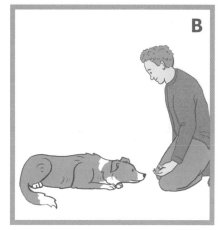

HOW TO TRAIN

1. Have the dog lie down. Sit or kneel in front of the dog. **(Refer to example A.)**

2. Hold a treat in front of your dog's nose and slowly move the treat toward the floor. When the dog follows the treat with their nose, click and reward. The goal is to have the dog touch the ground with their chin, so reward and praise the dog extra well when the dog does so. **(Refer to example B.)**

3. Repeat step 2 several times. When the dog consistently follows your hand toward the ground, you can stop rewarding for following your hand to the ground and only reward when the dog's chin touches the ground.

4. Add a voice command (for example, "head down" or "chin") each time the dog's chin touches the ground.

5. When the dog fully masters touching their chin to the ground, increase the duration of how long they keep their chin down. Instead of rewarding as soon as the dog's chin touches the ground, wait a second before clicking and rewarding. Slowly increase the duration (a few seconds per training session) until the dog can hold the position long enough for you to take a picture. If your dog knows the "stay" command, you can also use this to encourage them to hold the position until you say otherwise.

JUMP INTO OR ON ANY OBJECT/OFF

This trick can help build confidence and balance for dogs that are not sure-footed. It can also come in very handy, for example, at the vet or groomer, where the dog has to jump onto a table. But it's not limited to tables; you can train your dog to jump into a box, up on a hay bale, or onto your bed, for example. The reverse, off, is also useful for getting your pup out of places they shouldn't be, like your favorite chair.

NOT SUITABLE FOR

- Dogs with obesity or joint issues such as osteoarthritis, or dogs with short legs, for whom jumping up can be difficult, especially if the jump is high. Adjust the height of the object to your dog's ability.

WHAT YOU NEED

- Something stable for the dog to stand on
- Treats or a toy
- Clicker

HOW TO TRAIN

1. Choose an object that is large enough and strong enough for your dog to stand on it safely. It should be low enough to the ground that the dog can easily step on it.

2. Lure the dog onto it with a treat or toy that they like. Click and reward the dog well for standing on the object. Then lure the dog off the object, click and reward the dog for jumping off, and repeat. **(Refer to example A and B.)**

3. Some dogs may be a bit hesitant about jumping. If this is the case, try clicking and rewarding for one or two paws up on the object first. Repeat this several times, until the dog becomes more confident and starts offering the behavior on their own (this can take several days to several weeks). Only then can you start asking for the third and, finally, the fourth paw on the object.

CONTINUED...

4. When the dog understands what you want, add voice commands for both jumping on the object (for example, "up") and off the object ("off"). Say "up" when you see the dog is about to jump up on the object and "off" at the moment the dog jumps off; reward the dog well after each. Repeat this several times for multiple days, and try to reduce the luring a little bit each time you practice. Once mastered, you should be able to point at an object and have the dog jump up on command. **(Refer to example C.)**

5. Start asking for this behavior on all kinds of objects and surfaces, so long as they are stable and safe for the dog. This will help the dog build balance and confidence in jumping up. You can also choose to decrease the size of the object (slowly!), so the dog really has to place their paws close together in order to stand on the object. You can be as creative as you want! **(Refer to example D.)**

SPEAK/QUIET

Not only is it fun to have your dog speak on command, it can be used to train your dog to be quiet!

NOT SUITABLE FOR

- Some dogs who are not inclined to bark naturally. If this is the case with your dog, it will be very hard or maybe even impossible for them to learn this trick, and you shouldn't force it. Barking is a behavior that needs to be "marked," meaning you catch the behavior when the dog shows it on their own. For that reason, this trick is easier to teach when your dog is very vocal.

WHAT YOU NEED

- Treats or a toy
- Clicker

HOW TO TRAIN

SPEAK

1. The first step is to stimulate your dog to bark. Some dogs will bark out of excitement when exposed to a trigger that excites them, others when they see something that scares them or when they are anxious. For this training, it is important that the dog barks out of excitement, not anxiety or fear. When a dog is anxious or fearful, they might not be able to learn properly. Additionally, it will create a connection between barking and the feeling of being scared or anxious, which will make the trick unpleasant for the dog. However, when a dog is excited, that is a positive emotion, which will make learning this easier and more fun for the dog. (Refer to example A)

Try to make as little effort as possible to get your dog to bark. Many dogs will bark excitedly when someone knocks on the door, while others basically go insane. Knock on the door once so the dog will bark without going completely crazy.

2. When your dog barks, immediately say the voice command (for example, "speak"), click, and reward the dog. Make sure you praise the dog well for barking. (Refer to example B.)

CONTINUED...

3. Repeat steps 1 and 2, until you are confident the dog understands they are being rewarded for barking when you give the command.

4. When the dog seems to understand what you mean by "speak," you can remove the trigger and test to see if the dog will bark on voice command only. They may not bark right away but should bark within a couple of seconds. When the dog barks, praise them enthusiastically to make clear that was what you wanted. If your dog doesn't bark, try again later. **(Refer to example C.)**

5. Repeat step 4 until your dog always barks on command.

6. Now you can add a hand signal. While giving the dog the voice command, also give a hand signal. This hand signal should be very specific and not something you do every day. Some examples are tapping on your side with your hand or opening and closing your hand at a fast pace. Reward the dog well and repeat until the dog responds to this specific hand signal. **(Refer to example D.)**

TRAINING TIP: Do not reward your dog for barking when you did not ask for it! This will lead your dog to bark at random, which you do not want. Instead, ignore your dog when they bark when it is unwanted. This way, your dog will learn that barking only gets rewarded when you ask for it.

QUIET

Teaching a dog to bark is the first step to teaching a dog to be quiet. The reason for this is that when your dog can bark on command, they will bark when not excited, scared, or nervous about something. This makes it easier for the dog to focus on you and stop barking, as there is no trigger to keep barking at.

1. Ask your dog to bark and present them with a treat or toy. When they stop barking, say the voice command you want to use (for example, "quiet") and reward the dog. Make sure you say the command calmly; screaming will only excite your dog and cause them to bark more.

2. Repeat step 1. Make sure that every now and then you also reward the dog for barking on command. Otherwise, your dog may stop barking (or only bark once or twice) once they figure out they are being rewarded for being quiet.

3. Once you have repeated step 2 several times, you can test if your dog responds to the quiet command. Give the command while the dog is barking. If the dog stops barking (within about two seconds after giving the command), reward and praise the dog enthusiastically. If your dog continues to bark, repeat step 2 and try step 3 again later.

4. Repeat the above step until your dog stops barking at your command.

5. Once you tell your dog to be quiet, you don't want them to start barking again after a few seconds. Every time you practice this, increase the time between the dog being quiet and giving the reward. Start with one second of quiet and slowly increase the time to about five seconds or more. Reward and praise your dog each time. If your dog starts to bark after you give the command for quiet, wait a couple of seconds and try again.

6. If step 5 goes well, you can start practicing quiet in situations that usually trigger your dog's barking. Once the dog stops barking at the trigger (after you give the command for quiet), reward and praise immediately. Over time, increase the duration of the dog being quiet like you did in step 5.

7. In the end, your dog should be able to stop barking on command, without being rewarded for it each time (praising your dog with your voice when they follow a command is always okay).

TAKE A BOW

With these simple steps, you can teach your dog to take a bow. Your dog will learn to lower their front end, with the front paws stretched out and elbows touching the ground, while still standing up on their back legs.

COMMANDS/TRICKS YOUR DOG SHOULD KNOW

- Stand

WHAT YOU NEED

- Treats
- Clicker

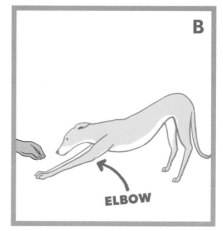

ELBOW

HOW TO TRAIN

1. Have the dog stand in front of you. Kneel so you are close to the ground and the dog. **(Refer to example A.)**

2. Hold a treat in front of the dog's nose and slowly lure them to the ground, so the dog has to lower themselves in order to reach the treat. Click and reward when the dog lowers their front end a bit (with the hind legs still standing) while following the treat.

3. When the dog starts to lower their front end, move your hand closer to the dog, so the dog has to go lower and lower until they touch the ground with their elbows. Click, reward, and praise your dog enthusiastically when they reach this point. **(Refer to example B.)**

4. The dog may lie down. If this happens, move your hand away from the dog, ask them to stand up, and try again.

5. Repeat step 3 until the dog takes a bow consistently without lying down.

6. Add a voice command (for example, "take a bow") each time your dog bows, and reward your dog well. Slowly decrease the amount of luring until your dog bows on voice command only.

BLOW BUBBLES

A fun and easy trick for the hot summer days.

WHAT YOU NEED

- A sturdy bowl
- Treats, preferably ones that sink in water
- Clicker

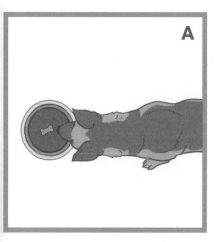

HOW TO TRAIN

1. Set down the bowl and put a treat in it. Have your dog take the treat from the bowl. Click and praise when the dog does so. Repeat this step a couple of times. **(Refer to example A.)**

2. Fill the bowl with a small amount of water and put the treat in it. Again, click and praise when the dog grabs the treat.

3. Every couple of repetitions, fill the bowl with a little more water, until the water depth is about one-third the length of the dog's nose.

4. Add a voice command (for example, "bubbles") each time the dog sticks their nose underwater. Repeat this several times, so the dog learns the connection between the nose being in the water and the word you're using.

5. Once the dog is comfortable with sticking their nose underwater, it is time to stop placing treats in the water, to test if the dog will put their nose in the water without them. If the dog doesn't fully stick their nose in the water but only touches the surface, this is fine. Click, reward, and praise the dog well when this happens. **(Refer to example B.)**

6. Repeat step 5 until the dog will fully stick their nose in the water on voice command.

CONTINUED...

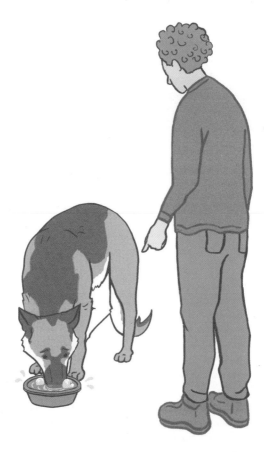

7. Now it is time to build duration. Wait a bit longer (start with half a second to one second) before clicking and rewarding the dog, and slowly increase the time every training session (the maximum will be around 3 seconds). You will see that, when the dog's nose is underwater, bubbles will start to form. Of course, dogs can't stay in this position for very long, so pay close attention to your dog and give them the freedom to lift their nose out of the bowl whenever they want. You have now taught your dog to blow bubbles!

INTERMEDIATE
DOG
TRICKS

When your dog rocks the beginner tricks, it is time to level up! The tricks in this chapter are more challenging, which means they will take more time and patience for your dog to learn. Some of them can be a bit harder on the dog's body and may require an extra bit of strength or balance. Make sure to watch your dog closely, and never ask your dog to do something they can't physically master or that causes them discomfort.

HOLD OR CARRY SOMETHING IN THE MOUTH/DROP IT

Most of us will know the feeling of missing that an extra hand—for example when bringing the groceries from the car to the house. Teaching your dog to carry things in their mouth not only means your dog will know another cool trick, it can come in handy! Of course, there is no point in having your dog hold or carry objects for you if they don't let it go when you ask for it. This is why I have included training for "drop it" here too.

WHAT YOU NEED

- Two toys
- Treats
- Clicker

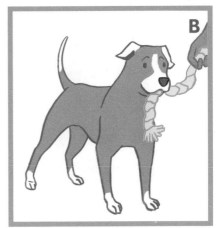

HOW TO TRAIN

HOLD OR CARRY SOMETHING IN THE MOUTH

1. You will need a toy your dog really likes, as well as treats. Hold the toy in your hand and wiggle it around to catch your dog's attention. If this doesn't work, try throwing the toy a small distance to encourage your dog to chase and catch it. When your dog shows interest in the toy by sniffing—or, even better, biting—click and reward. Repeat this step several times and praise the dog enthusiastically when they grab the toy with their mouth. **(Refer to example A and B.)**

2. When the dog consistently grabs the toy with their mouth, start building duration. Do not click and reward immediately when the dog grabs the toy, but instead wait a second.

If the dog doesn't hold onto the toy, it can help to tug at it a bit. This usually stimulates a dog to hold on and pull back. At first, reward whenever the dog tugs at the toy. When this goes well, try to stop tugging for half a second to one second and, if the dog still has the toy in their mouth, click, praise, and reward them well.

3. Repeat steps 1 and 2, and slowly, over the course of several training sessions, increase the time your dog has to hold the toy in their mouth without pulling or tugging at it.

CONTINUED...

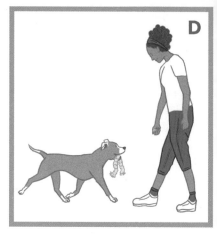

4. When this goes well, start to move your hands off the toy for a short moment before putting your hands back on it. Click, reward, and praise the dog well when they don't drop the toy. It is probably easiest if your dog sits down for this step. **(Refer to example C.)**

5. Practice step 4 several times, and start adding a voice command (for example, "hold (it)") each time your dog holds the toy in their mouth. Make sure you don't click or praise the dog after they drop the toy, because then you are rewarding the dog for letting it go, and they may come to associate "hold (it)" with dropping the toy. It is best if you take the toy from the dog when you are going to reward instead of having the dog drop the toy on the ground, as this will stimulate the dog to hold onto it until you say otherwise.

6. When the dog understands what is wanted from them, switch up the item the dog has to hold in their mouth. Start with different toys and other soft objects, and slowly move to smaller objects or those that are more difficult to hold, like a set of keys. If the dog is uncomfortable with holding a certain item, repeat all the above steps for that specific item to see if the dog becomes more comfortable with doing it.

7. The last step is getting your dog to walk with the object in their mouth. When the dog is holding it, take a few steps back (not too far in the beginning) and call the dog toward you. Reward and praise the dog when they hold onto the toy while walking. **(Refer to example D.)**

TEACH YOUR DOG CRAZY TRICKS

DROP IT

1. For this you will need either one toy and treats or two toys. The first step is to get the dog to grab the first toy with their mouth. To achieve this, you can use the first step(s) for teaching "hold (it)."

2. When the dog has the toy, hold a treat in front of their nose or show the other toy (move it around to make it more interesting for the dog). In order to grab the treat or other toy, your dog must drop the first toy. When the dog lets go of the toy, immediately click and reward. **(Refer to example E.)**

3. If you only have one toy, give it back to the dog. Repeat step 2 several times, until the dog drops the toy consistently when offered a treat or another toy.

4. Add a voice command (for example, "drop (it)," "leave (it)," or "out") each time the dog lets go of the toy. **(Refer to example F.)**

5. The last step is to get the dog to drop the toy without offering food or another toy as a trade. Say the voice command without showing the treat or second toy. When the dog drops the toy, click, praise, and reward them well. If the dog doesn't drop the toy, wait a couple of seconds before showing the treat or second toy again. Over the next several training sessions, increase that time, so the dog learns to drop the toy with a voice command before a treat or a second toy comes out. Repeat until the dog fully masters the "drop (it)" command without the need of a trade.

FETCH AND RETRIEVE AN OBJECT BY NAME

How great would it be if your dog could fetch the remote, your keys, or your phone on command? For some dogs, like most retrievers, fetching comes naturally, but any dog can be taught this trick.

COMMANDS/TRICKS YOUR DOG SHOULD KNOW

- Hold or Carry Something in the Mouth/Drop It (page 70)

WHAT YOU NEED

- Toy
- Treats
- Clicker

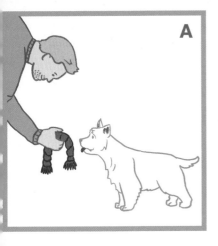

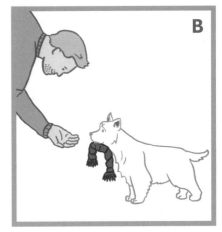

HOW TO TRAIN

1. Hold the toy in your hand, stretch your hand out toward the dog, and tell the dog to hold it. Click and when the dog takes the toy from your hand reward with a treat. **(Refer to example A.)**

2. Repeat step 1 several times, each time lowering your hand toward the ground. At a certain point, your dog should be able to take the toy from the ground with you just pointing at it. **(Refer to example B.)**

3. Once the dog takes the toy from the ground, add a voice command (for example, "get it" or "fetch") each time the dog takes the toy from the ground. Later on, you can use different commands for each object, but for now a general command is best.

4. Once you are confident the dog understands the command, slowly start to increase the distance between you and your dog while having your dog fetch the toy. Call your dog toward you each time and reward them for bringing the toy to you, so the dog learns that they only get a reward when you have the toy. Make sure the dog doesn't drop the toy when they give it to you.

5. Once the dog successfully retrieves the toy from a distance each time you ask, start to throw the toy away from you and then have the dog fetch it. Reward the dog well the first few times they retrieve the toy. You have now taught your dog a basic fetch.

CONTINUED...

6. You can start to vary the object your dog has to retrieve. Begin with different toys and slowly move to other random (but safe) objects. You can throw them or have your dog fetch an object that is already lying somewhere (as long as you have made clear that is the object your dog needs to fetch). The first step for this is to teach the dog the name of each object. Have your dog hold the object (like the remote) and repeat the object's name several times while the dog continues to hold it. Then praise and reward the dog well. Repeat this several times. **(Refer to example C.)**

7. Now either throw the object or make sure it is in a place it is usually found (for something like the remote), and follow steps 1 through 4, adding the word for that specific object each time you give the command. For instance, you would say "get the remote" instead of just "get it." Repeat these steps several times, until (1) you are positive the dog understands the link between the object's name and the object itself, and (2) the dog successfully fetches the object every time you ask. **(Refer to example D.)**

8. Once the dog consistently fetches the specific object from its usual place without any mistakes, you can start to move the object around so the dog has to search for it. Make sure you reward and praise the dog well each time the object is retrieved.

CATCH A FRISBEE

Have you ever seen a dog chase down and catch a Frisbee in midair? It's an awesome trick and kicks up the standard "fetch" to a new level.

NOT SUITABLE FOR

- Puppies, still-growing young dogs, and those with joint issues like osteo-arthritis or obesity, as it puts extra pressure on the joints.

COMMANDS/TRICKS YOUR DOG SHOULD KNOW

- Fetch and Retrieve an Object by Name (page 74)
- Walk Around a Person/Object (page 24) is also useful to know

WHAT YOU NEED

- Frisbee made specifically for dogs

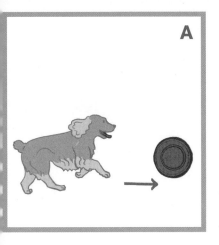

HOW TO TRAIN

1. To start, you will have to get your dog interested in the Frisbee. Instead of throwing it in the air, throw it downward so that it rolls on the ground like a wheel. Most dogs love to chase things, and this is an easy transition from the basic fetch. Because the Frisbee is on the ground, it is easy for the dog to locate it and catch it. To make it even easier for the dog to locate the Frisbee, ask them to walk around you right before you throw it. This way, the dog will be facing in the direction that the Frisbee is heading, as well as already walking or running at the moment you throw it. Make sure you don't wait too long before throwing the Frisbee, as there is a chance the dog will have already turned back around toward you, meaning it will have to turn around again to go after the Frisbee. **(Refer to example A.)**

2. In the beginning, the Frisbee will probably fall over on its side before the dog is able to grab it. When the dog does manage to catch the Frisbee while it is still rolling, reward and praise them well.

3. Repeat steps 1 and 2 until the dog frequently catches the Frisbee while it is still rolling.

4. Now it is time to teach the dog to catch the Frisbee when it is held in a horizontal position. Hold the Frisbee in your hand and slowly move it away from the dog, while keeping it at your dog's nose height. Encourage the dog to grab the Frisbee. When the dog grabs it, reward them well and let the Frisbee go. **(Refer to example B.)**

CONTINUED...

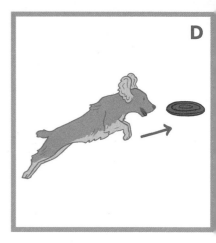

5. Repeat step 4, slowly increasing your speed so that at some point, the dog will have to run to grab the Frisbee. Try to move as little as possible yourself, running or twirling in a small circle with your dog on the outside of the circle.

6. When your dog is grabbing the Frisbee consistently, start increasing its height to the point where the dog has to jump to catch the Frisbee. For some dogs this may be a bit difficult in the beginning, so be patient. When the dog jumps and catches it, reward and praise the dog well. **(Refer to example C.)**

7. Once the dog is consistently jumping up to grab the Frisbee, you can start throwing it. Repeat step 6, but now throw the Frisbee right before the dog jumps. Make sure to throw it to where the dog would normally catch the Frisbee. If you throw it too fast, too slow, too high, or too low, the dog will not be able to catch it.

8. If step 7 goes well, slowly start to work on throwing the Frisbee farther away (small steps!). Depending on how fast and athletic your dog is and how good your throwing technique is, progress can be really fast or take a very long time. Either way, be patient and enjoy the playtime with your dog! **(Refer to example D.)**

TRAINING TIP: It is a good idea to practice throwing a Frisbee without a dog before doing this with your dog. Knowing how to throw it smoothly will make it a lot easier and safer for the dog to catch it while it is flying. Practice throwing in different directions and at different speeds, and try hitting targets with the Frisbee to improve your aim. Yes, that's right—sometimes you need to train yourself before you can train your dog!

ACT ASHAMED OR EMBARRASSED

This trick is great fun. When friends or family (or your pup) does something silly or makes a mistake, have your dog cover their face with a paw, as if ashamed or embarrassed, on command.

COMMANDS/TRICKS YOUR DOG SHOULD KNOW

- Sit
- Stay can also be useful

WHAT YOU NEED

- Treats
- Clicker
- A sticky note, sticker, tape, or something else that is sticky (should not be too sticky!)

TEACH YOUR DOG CRAZY TRICKS

HOW TO TRAIN

1. Sit or kneel and have the dog sit in front of you. Hold the clicker in one hand and a treat in the other. **(Refer to example A.)**

2. Put the sticky note, sticker, tape, or something else that works for you on your dog's nose (for convenience, this will be called a sticker for the rest of this explanation). Make sure you use something that isn't too sticky, so it will come off easily without hurting the dog. **(Refer to example B.)**

3. Most dogs will find the feeling of something sticking to their nose annoying, which will cause them to paw at their nose. Closely observe your dog and immediately click when the dog touches their nose with a paw. Try not to click too early or too late; you want to specifically mark the moment the dog's paw touches the nose. Reward and praise the dog well, and repeat steps 2 and 3 several times (over multiple training sessions). Remove the sticker regularly to give the dog a break and avoid becoming frustrated. It can take a while, but eventually, your dog will learn they are rewarded when they paw at their nose. **(Refer to example C.)**

CONTINUED...

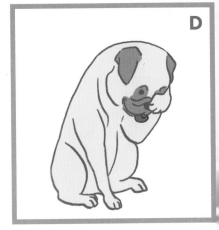

4. Add a voice command (for example, "shame on you" or "ashamed") each time your dog is about to touch their nose with a paw.

5. Repeat steps 2 through 4, until you feel the dog understands the behavior being asked of them.

6. Now remove the sticker to test if your dog will touch their nose on command. Wait a couple of seconds for your dog to respond. Most dogs will act a bit confused, so give them some time to think. If the dog doesn't show the desired behavior, place the sticker back on their nose, repeat the above steps a few times, then try it without the sticker again. When the dog does touch their nose with a paw (even if it is for a split second), click, reward, and praise your dog enthusiastically. Repeat this until the dog consistently touches their nose with a paw.

7. Now slowly work on duration. Most dogs will swipe a paw over their nose, but what is desired is to have the dog hold its paw still over their nose. Ask for the "shame" behavior, and wait until your dog touches their nose for one second or longer. At this point it isn't necessary for the dog to hold their paw completely still. Click, praise, reward the dog well, and try again. **(Refer to example D.)**

8. Over the course of multiple training sessions (this might take weeks), increase the time your dog has to keep a paw on their nose to receive a treat. Over time, your dog will learn to keep their paw still and hold the position. Here it can also help to give a "stay" command, if your dog is familiar with this.

TRAINING TIP:

There is a chance your dog won't respond to the sticker on their nose. For those dogs, it may work to gently blow in their face. Many dogs don't like this, and it might lead them to paw at their face.

SIT PRETTY

Not only is "sit pretty" an adorable trick, it is also a good core strength and balance exercise for your dog. This trick is the basis of many other tricks in this book.

NOT SUITABLE FOR

- Young dogs or dogs with joint issues, as this trick requires a fair bit of strength and balance to hold the position. For these dogs, it is important to build up duration slowly and to keep training sessions short. This will also give your dog the time to work out which position of sit pretty works best for them (some dogs like to keep their front paws in a low position, while others stick them all the way up in the air, for example).

COMMANDS/TRICKS YOUR DOG SHOULD KNOW

- Sit

WHAT YOU NEED

- Treats
- Clicker

HOW TO TRAIN

1. Have the dog sit in front of you. Depending on the size of your dog, you can choose to kneel, sit, or stand. **(Refer to example A.)**

2. Take a treat and hold it right above your dog's nose. Once they are interested in the treat, slowly raise the treat up to a height your dog can't reach with their nose when in a normal sitting position. Wait for your dog to lift their front paws off the ground to reach the treat. Click right at the moment the front paws are in the air and reward the dog well. **(Refer to example B.)**

3. Repeat step 2, each time holding the treat a bit higher, until the dog has to fully shift their weight onto their back end in order to reach the treat. The dog's back should be in a vertically straight position.

4. Once the dog is consistently able to achieve this position, work on duration. Lure your dog into the position and wait one second before clicking and rewarding. Holding this position requires a lot of strength and balance, so increase the duration slowly over the course of multiple training sessions. There might be times when the dog holds the position well, then sits back down the next. This is usually the result of your dog trying to learn how to keep its balance. Ignore it when your dog sits back down too quickly and just keep on practicing. **(Refer to example C.)**

CONTINUED...

If you notice that your dog is sitting down faster than usual or their hind legs are shaking, your dog is tired. Stop the training and repeat again on another day. This usually also means that your training sessions are too long, so shorten them. Five minutes is usually long enough for one training session of this trick.

5. Once the dog can stay in the sit pretty position for a couple of seconds, add a voice command (for example, "sit pretty" or "beg") each time your dog sits pretty. While teaching your dog the voice command, reduce the hand luring.

6. When your dog fully masters this trick, they should be able to sit pretty for at least five seconds on voice command only. **(Refer to example D.)**

WALK ON TWO HIND LEGS

Dogs walking like humans always seem to amaze people. And it sure is an impressive trick!

NOT SUITABLE FOR

- Dogs with osteoarthritis, hip dysplasia, or other joint problems, as well as obese dogs, as this trick will put a lot of extra pressure on the dog's hind-quarters and back. It is also not suitable for puppies or growing young dogs and may be extra difficult for dogs with shorter legs. This trick is not recommended for large and giant dogs.

COMMANDS/TRICKS YOUR DOG SHOULD KNOW

- Stand
- It is a good idea to first teach Sit Pretty (page 86) for balance training and to build up strength. Also, if you teach this trick first, it may be harder to teach Sit Pretty because your dog may be more inclined to stand up instead of sitting with their paws up.

WHAT YOU NEED

- Treats
- Clicker

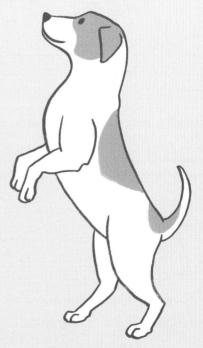

HOW TO TRAIN

1. Have your dog stand in front of you while standing yourself. If your dog knows sit pretty, you could use this as a starting position as well. **(Refer to example A.)**

2. Hold a treat in front of your dog's nose and move it toward the back of their head at a height your dog cannot reach while standing with all four paws on the ground or while sitting pretty. When the dog lifts their front paws off the ground or stands up (from sitting pretty) in order to reach the treat, click, reward, and praise the dog enthusiastically. If your dog doesn't follow the treat, try to move it around above the dog's head and nose in order to catch their attention. Most dogs will jump for the treat at some point (also make sure it is something they really like and want!). **(Refer to example B.)**

3. Repeat step 2, and raise the treat a bit higher with each training session until the dog has to stand up straight. Make sure your dog only lifts their front paws and doesn't jump up with all four paws off the ground. If your dog jumps, ignore and do not click or reward the behavior. Soon your dog will understand that jumping isn't going to get them the treat.

4. Once your dog is consistently standing up with their front paws off the ground, add a voice command (for example, "walk" or "straight") each time the dog stands up.

CONTINUED...

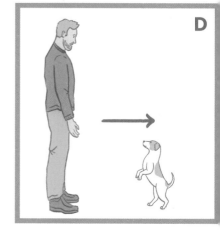

5. Standing still on their hind legs is very difficult for a dog. Walking backward is the easiest way for a dog to balance this way. Instead of rewarding the dog directly when standing on their hind legs, slowly walk toward the dog with the treat until the dog takes a step backward. Immediately click, reward, and praise the dog when this happens. **(Refer to example C.)**

6. Repeat steps 4 and 5. Every couple of training sessions, you can ask for one extra step backward, until the dog can walk backward on their hind legs for several steps. Some dogs will need more training sessions for that extra step than others (smaller dogs will usually be able to do this faster than larger, heavier dogs). The dog needs to build the right muscles to keep this up for a longer period of time, so give your dog the time to do this and follow their pace.

7. Over time you can slowly remove the hand lure and increase the distance. This will take time and patience, so do not rush it. Before you know it, your dog will be able to walk on two feet. **(Refer to example D.)**

TAKE IT UP A NOTCH: You can also teach your dog to walk forward. However, this is a lot more difficult for the dog. To teach it, instead of luring the dog backward and walking toward the dog, walk backward and lure the dog toward you.

HUG

What's cuter than having your dog hug you? There are multiple ways to teach this; my method is suitable for all dogs, including small dogs and dogs that do not like to be touched or held close. Following these steps, you will teach your dog to hug/hold your leg with their front paws. You can use this same technique to teach your dog to hug you by laying their paws on your shoulders.

COMMANDS/ TRICKS YOUR DOG SHOULD KNOW

- Sit
- Give Paw (page 18)
- Sit Pretty (page 86)

WHAT YOU NEED

- A soft object for your dog to hold, like a pool noodle
- Treats
- Clicker

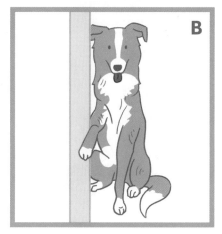

HOW TO TRAIN

1. Sit and have the dog sit down next to you.

2. With one hand, hold the object in front of the dog, close to their chest in a vertical position, and ask for a paw with your other hand. Instead of having your dog touch your hand with a paw, hold your hand close to the object so the dog touches the object instead. Click, reward, and praise the dog when they touch the object. **(Refer to example A.)**

3. Repeat step 2 until the dog understands to touch the object. The goal is to have the dog touch the object with the inside of their paw. When this happens, reward and praise the dog enthusiastically. If your dog doesn't show this behavior, try delaying the reward for touching the object. Most dogs will start to scratch the object out of impatience, which will result in the dog touching it with the inside of their paw. **(Refer to example B.)**

CONTINUED...

4. If step 3 goes well, ask your dog to sit pretty. When the dog sits pretty, place the object between the dog's paws, close to the chest, and ask for a paw. When the dog touches the object with the inside of their paw, click and reward the dog well. Start with rewarding for one paw, and, if that goes well after several repetitions, wait for the second paw to touch the object and reward for that.

5. If the dog touches the object with both paws, you can start to add a voice command (for example, "hug" or "both paws") each time they touch the object with the inside of both paws. Meanwhile, reduce the hand luring so the dog learns to hug on voice command only. **(Refer to example C.)**

6. The next step is to hold the position longer. Once the dog is touching the object with both paws, very gently pull at the object. This will automatically make most dogs hold on to it tighter.

7. If the above steps go well, stand up and ask your dog to hold your leg with both paws, following the directions in step 4. At first, they may be confused by your standing up, so it is okay to use a food lure the first few times you practice this. Make sure your dog stays sitting down and does not stand up, as this will look way less cute. **(Refer to example D.)**

SAY YOUR PRAYERS

Have your dog place their front paws on your arm or a table and stick their nose in between, like they are praying.

COMMANDS/TRICKS YOUR DOG SHOULD KNOW

- Sit
- Sit Pretty (page 86) is recommended

WHAT YOU NEED

- Treats
- Clicker

A

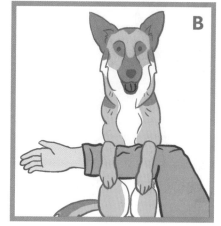

B

HOW TO TRAIN

1. Kneel and have your dog sit next to you. Hold a clicker in one hand and a treat in the other.

2. Ask your dog to sit pretty. **(Refer to example A.)**

3. Once the dog lifts up both front paws, move your arm (the one you are holding the clicker with) underneath them (in a horizontal position) so the dog lands on your arm with both front paws. Click, reward, and praise the dog enthusiastically for touching your arm with both front paws.

4. Repeat steps 2 and 3 several times, until you are confident the dog understands that they have to place their front paws on your arm. Slowly stop moving your arm under the dog's paws, so they have to place their paws on your arm by themselves. Make sure the dog doesn't stand up while practicing this trick. **(Refer to example B.)**

5. Once the above step goes well, work on duration so the dog learns to keep their paws on your arm and not jump back down right away. Wait a second longer before rewarding the dog. Repeat this and slowly increase the time, until the dog can hold the position for at least five seconds.

CONTINUED...

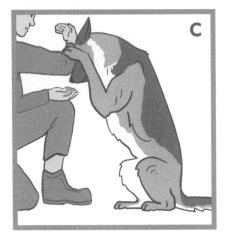

6. It is time to start luring the dog's nose down between their paws. Hold a treat between the dog's front paws, coming from underneath your arm. Do this with the hand that is still free. Once the dog looks down toward the treat, click, reward, and praise the dog. Most dogs will remove their paws from your arm the first time this is asked. When this happens, place the dog's paws on your arm again and try again. Soon the dog will learn that putting their paws down isn't going to get them the treat. **(Refer to example C.)**

7. Repeat step 6, each time holding the treat lower as well as slightly closer toward you, until finally the dog has to fully stick their head between their paws to get to the treat. Click, reward, and praise your dog enthusiastically for this.

8. Once your dog is reliably doing this, add a voice command (for example, "say your prayers") each time your dog sticks their head in between their front paws. **(Refer to example D.)**

9. Once the dog performs the trick on voice command with minimal luring, work on duration. Each time the dog performs the trick, wait a bit longer with the reward. Repeat this until your dog can hold the position for about five seconds.

YOUR FEET ON MINE!

With this trick, you will teach your dog to stand between your legs, facing forward and placing both front paws on your feet. Your dog should be comfortable with standing between your legs to perform this trick.

WHAT YOU NEED

- Treats
- Clicker

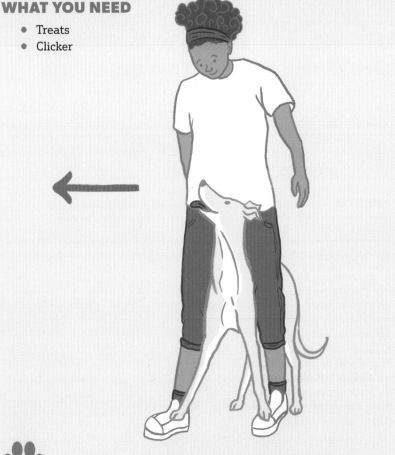

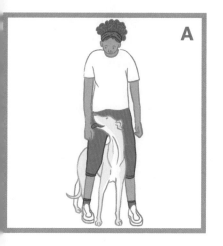

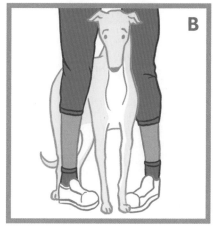

HOW TO TRAIN

1. Lure the dog in between your legs from the back, so you are both facing forward. Click and reward when the dog stands between your legs. Do not focus on where the dog positions their front feet yet. **(Refer to example A.)**

2. Repeat step 1 several times, then add a voice command (for example, "under" or "between") each time your dog stands between your legs.

3. Now you're going to focus on the feet. Turn your feet inward so the tips of your shoes almost touch. Make sure the shoes you wear provide a bit of grip at the top, as anything slippery or round will make the dog's paws slide off. It also helps to wear large shoes, so it is easier for the dog to target your feet. **(Refer to example B.)**

4. Have the dog stand between your legs. Because your feet are now in the way of where the dog will have to stand, there is a good chance your dog will step on your feet with at least one paw. Click and reward as soon as one of the dog's paws touches your feet. **(Refer to example C.)**

5. Keep clicking and rewarding the dog for stepping on your feet with one paw. Two paws are even better, so, if this happens, reward and praise your dog extra well so they know they did something fantastic!

CONTINUED...

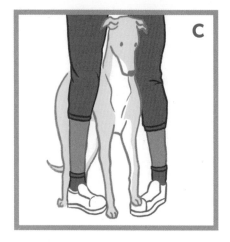

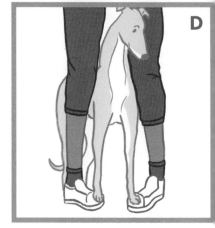

6. When the dog consistently steps on your feet with a paw, it is time to wait for the second paw before rewarding them. Wait for your dog to figure out what to do to get the treat. Most likely your dog will start to move around with their front paws, eventually stepping on your feet with both paws. Again, reward and praise your dog enthusiastically when this happens. **(Refer to example D.)**

Some dogs will figure this out in no time; others will need longer to think about what needs to be done. This is okay. Give the dog some time to work it out, and ignore the mistakes that will be made.

7. Once the foot placement goes well each time you ask, it is time to work on duration, as well as a command. Say a voice command (for example, "feet") each time the dog steps on your feet with both paws. Meanwhile, wait a little longer with the reward each time to build duration. The dog should be able to hold the position for around ten seconds when they master this trick.

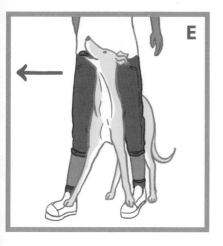

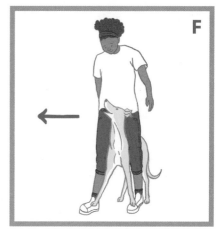

8. Finally, you can work to correct foot placement. Instead of keeping your feet close together (which, in all honestly, is not a comfortable position), slowly move your feet to a more normal standing position. Make sure, however, that your feet still point in a little and your legs are as close together as possible. Your dog should be able to perform this trick without having to "split" their front legs apart, as this can be very bad for them. **(Refer to example E.)**

9. When the dog can hold the position for several seconds, it is time to start walking. Step-by-step. Get the dog into position, and gently lift up one foot just high enough to be able to move it forward and put it back down. In the beginning, it will look more like shuffling than walking. The first time you do this, it may feel weird for the dog, and they may step away. Ask the dog to move back into position and try again. Be enthusiastic and positive to encourage them to trust you. **(Refer to example F.)**

10. Repeat steps 8 and 9, and each time a certain number of steps goes well, add some more.

11. When your dog masters this trick, you should be able to walk with them standing on your feet with both front paws.

CLOSE THE DOOR

Did someone forget to close the door? How great would it be if the dog could do it for you?! This trick is only suitable for doors that can be easily pushed closed.

WHAT YOU NEED

- Treats
- Clicker
- Sticky notes

A

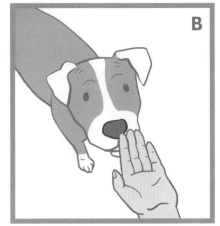

B

HOW TO TRAIN

1. The first step is to target train your dog, meaning you will teach the dog to touch something with their nose on command. We are going to start with your hand. Hold your hand flat, lay a treat in your palm, and secure it with your thumb, so your hand is still flat but the treat can't fall on the ground. Hold your hand in front of the dog's nose and wait for your dog to touch your hand with their nose. When they do that, click and give the treat. **(Refer to example A.)**

2. Repeat step 1 several times, then add a voice command (for example, "touch") each time the dog touches your hand with their nose.

3. Now remove the treat from your hand and try again. When the dog touches your hand, again click and reward. Repeat this step until your dog touches your hand on command at any time, without you having to hold a treat. **(Refer to example B.)**

CONTINUED...

4. Put a sticky note on the palm of your hand, hold your hand close to a door (so that the back of your hand touches the door), and ask your dog to touch it. Reward the dog well for doing this. Repeat this a couple of times. **(Refer to example C.)**

5. Remove the sticky note from your hand and stick it to the door. Point at the sticky note and ask your dog to touch it. Reward the dog very well when they touch the note with their nose. **(Refer to example D.)**

6. Once your dog will reliably touch the sticky note on the door, you can open the door slightly. Keep asking your dog to touch the sticky note until the door moves. Click as soon as the door moves and reward the dog well, so they know they did something right (it can be a bit weird for the dog at first when the door starts moving). **(Refer to example E.)**

7. Repeat step 6 until the dog manages to shut the door. Click, reward, and praise the dog enthusiastically when this happens.

8. Repeat step 7, adding a voice command (for example, "close the door") each time the dog closes the door.

9. Now see if the dog will close the door without it having the sticky note on it. Remove the sticky note from the door and ask the dog to close it. Reward and praise the dog well when they touch the door with their nose without the sticky note being on it. **(Refer to example F.)**

10. Keep practicing, and, with each training session, open the door a little wider until the dog can close a door that is all the way open.

SAY YES/SAY NO

Teach your dog to answer your questions by shaking no or nodding yes with their head.

COMMANDS/TRICKS YOUR DOG SHOULD KNOW

- Sit

WHAT YOU NEED

- Treats

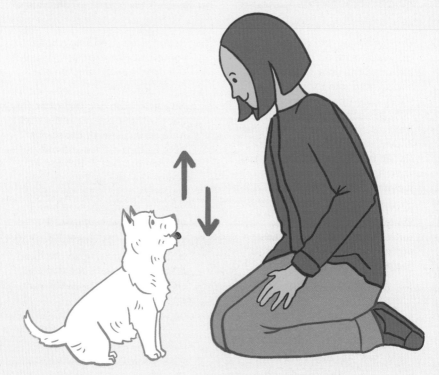

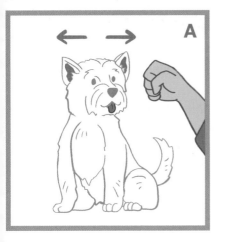

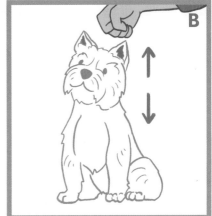

HOW TO TRAIN

1. Ask your dog to sit. Kneel in front of the dog.

2. Hold a treat in your hand and close your hand in a fist.

For no: Move the fist from the left side of the dog's face to the right side and reward the dog when they follow the fist with their nose. **(Refer to example A.)**

For yes: Do the same thing as for teaching no, but instead move your fist up and down. **(Refer to example B.)**

3. Repeat step 2 several times and reward each time the dog follows the fist. Once this goes well, add a voice command. Most dogs will recognize the word "yes" as "hey, I did something good" and "no" as "oh, I did something not good," so try

to avoid these words. Instead, you can say these words in a different language—in Dutch we say "ja" and "nee," for example—or try a twist on the words so they sound differently, like "yep" and "nope."

4. When the dog is reliably following your commands, begin to slowly move your fist away from the dog. Keep rewarding when the dog shakes their nose from left to right (for no) or up and down (for yes).

5. Continue to move your hand away from the dog, and work on minimizing the hand signals over time. For most dogs, it will take quite some time before they know how to shake no or nod yes on voice command only or with a minimal hand signal.

JUMP THROUGH A HOOP

A classic "crazy" trick that will make you feel like your backyard is a circus tent.

NOT SUITABLE FOR

- Dogs with osteoarthritis, elbow or hip dysplasia, or other joint problems. Also, not puppies and young growing dogs, as it can negatively affect growth.

WHAT YOU NEED

- A hula hoop that is large enough for your dog to jump through (the hoop should be taller than the dog)
- Treats or a toy

TRAINING TIP: You can also teach your dog to jump through the hoop by placing your arms around the hoop. Have your dog jump through the hoop like that several times. Then remove the hoop so the dog jumps through your arms!

TEACH YOUR DOG CRAZY TRICKS

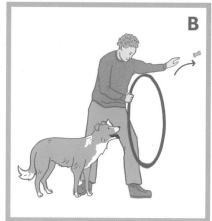

HOW TO TRAIN

1. Kneel and hold the hoop upright with one hand in front of the dog, resting it on the floor. Hold a treat or toy in your other hand and lure the dog through the hoop. **(Refer to example A.)**

2. Repeat step 1 a couple of times, until the dog walks through the hoop without any hesitation.

3. Now only lure the dog with the reward until their nose is sticking through the hoop, then throw the reward in the direction the dog is heading. **(Refer to example B.)**

4. Repeat step 3 until the dog walks through the hoop without any hesitation to follow the reward. Now slowly raise the hoop off the ground, starting

with just an inch. When the dog shows they are comfortable with that increase, continue lifting it an inch or two at a time.

5. Once the dog has to jump in order to go after the reward, you have reached the right height!

6. Make sure not to hold the hoop too high, which will increase the chance of injury.

7. Now add a voice command (for example, "hoop" or "through") each time the dog jumps through the hoop. After a while, try to have your dog jump through the hoop on voice command only. Reward and praise the dog enthusiastically when they do this.

ADVANCED DOG TRICKS

Congratulations, you are really leveling up! These tricks are both harder to teach and harder to learn, so patience is needed. Some of them are a combination of several tricks that together make one trick. Because of their increased difficulty, you will find more tricks that are not suitable for all dogs. However, there are still plenty left that can be performed by all types of dogs.

PERFORM TRICKS WHILE FACING AWAY FROM YOU

Most people stop trick training after their dog performs a trick right in front of them. But having your dog perform tricks while facing the other direction is a whole different thing. As your dog can't see you (and you can't use hand signals or lures), they have to fully trust you and understand everything you say. This is the ultimate test of how well you have trained your dog. And it looks so cool!

COMMANDS/ TRICKS YOUR DOG SHOULD KNOW

- Stand
- Whatever trick(s) you like

WHAT YOU NEED

- Treats
- Clicker

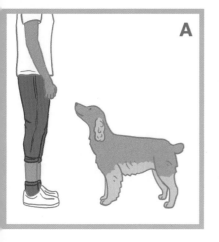

HOW TO TRAIN

1. Have your dog stand in front of you. **(Refer to example A.)**

2. Hold a treat in front of the dog's nose and lure them to make a half turn away from you, the dog stopping with their hind end closest to you. Click and reward the dog. Repeat this several times, so the dog understands that they are being rewarded for facing away from you. **(Refer to example B.)**

3. Slowly start to increase the time your dog has to stand with their back to you. Do this by waiting a second before you click and reward the dog, then increasing the delay for the treat. If the dog turns around before you've offered the treat, ignore the behavior and ask the dog to turn around. Make sure you don't increase the time too fast; this will help prevent the dog from turning around too soon.

Make sure the dog is looking forward or upward each time you click and reward. This trick doesn't look as good if the dog is looking behind at you.

CONTINUED...

4. Add a voice command (for example, "half") each time your dog faces away from you. This way, the dog will learn to make half a turn on command. Slowly increase your distance from the dog as well, so the dog learns to turn around no matter how close or far away they are from you. **(Refer to example C.)**

5. Once the dog masters the half turn, you can add a trick they have to perform while facing away from you. Start with one your dog knows really well on a voice command. As this is new for the dog, they will most likely turn around the first few times they are asked to do the trick in this position. Use luring to help the dog understand that it is okay to perform the trick without facing you. If the dog does turn around, ignore this and ask them to try it again. When the dog does perform the trick while facing the other way (even if it is an easy trick the dog knows well), reward and praise the dog enthusiastically to let them know they did a great job. This will help build trust and encourage the dog to do it again. **(Refer to example D.)**

SIT PRETTY!

6. Slowly decrease the luring until the dog will perform the trick facing away from you on voice command only.

WHERE'S YOUR BUM?

As far as I'm concerned, you can never teach your dog enough weird tricks. For this one, have your dog turn around and bow in front of you, showing you their bum, on command. This trick is quite similar to Perform Tricks While Facing Away from You, but now we are going to combine two tricks into one.

COMMANDS/TRICKS YOUR DOG SHOULD KNOW

- Take a Bow (page 62)
- Perform Tricks While Facing Away from You (page 116)

WHAT YOU NEED

- Treats
- Clicker

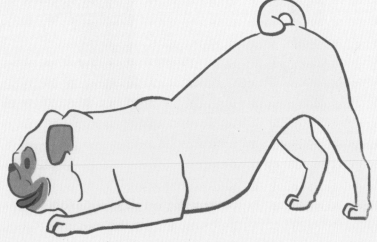

HOW TO TRAIN

1. If your dog hasn't performed take a bow facing away from you before, teach this trick first.

2. Once that goes well, the dog should be able to (1) turn around on command, and (2) bow on command facing away from you. For this trick, you want the dog to execute these two behaviors with just one command. Right after you have given the dog the voice command to bow, say the new command you will use for this trick (for example, "show me your bum"). Click and reward the dog well when they bow in front of you.

3. Repeat step 2 multiple times, each time saying the bow command and the new command. After a while, remove the bow command and see if the dog will take a bow on the new command. Click, reward, and praise the dog enthusiastically if they do this. If the dog doesn't take a bow, repeat step 2 a few times more and try again.

4. Make sure that with every repetition, your dog has to turn around and take a bow, so the dog learns the connection between these two tricks. Also, switch up the trick the dog has to perform while facing away from you every now and then, so they learn that taking a bow is not the only trick they ever have to do in that position.

5. Once your dog will take a bow following only the new voice command, it is time to remove the command for "turning around" as well. At the start, you may have to help the dog a bit with luring. Give the dog the "show me your bum" command, and if the dog doesn't turn around on their own, lure them into position.

6. Repeat step 5 for several training sessions. It will most likely take a while for your dog to understand this trick on voice command only, and it will go faster if small steps are taken. Every couple of training sessions, try to reduce the luring so the dog has to think on their own more and more.

7. Finally, the dog should turn around and take a bow following the one command.

TWIST AND TURN WHILE STANDING ON HIND LEGS

Once you train your dog to walk on their hind legs, the next step is to teach them to spin around while standing on two legs!

NOT SUITABLE FOR

- Puppies or growing young dogs, as well as elderly dogs and those with obesity or joint issues, including hip dysplasia, spondylosis, and osteoarthritis. It is also not recommended for large or giant dogs. Make sure your dog is in good health before you start training for this trick.

COMMANDS/ TRICKS YOUR DOG SHOULD KNOW

- Walk on Two Hind Legs (page 90)

WHAT YOU NEED

- Treats

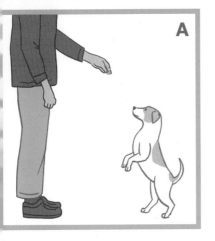

HOW TO TRAIN

1. Before teaching this trick, your dog should have fully mastered walking on hind legs and be able to do it for at least five seconds. Only then can you start working on spinning around.

2. Ask your dog to stand on their hind legs. Hold a treat in your hand and keep it in front of your dog's nose. **(Refer to example A.)**

3. Move the hand with the treat to the side of the dog's head. Move slowly at first, so the dog can easily follow your hand. The dog now has to make a quarter of a circle. Repeat this step a couple of times. **(Refer to example B.)**

4. When your dog has mastered step 3, you can slowly move toward turning around half a circle, then slowly but surely move toward a full circle (this will take multiple training sessions to achieve).

Closely observe your dog when teaching this trick. When they have trouble turning around while standing on their hind legs (they are not able to keep standing, or they are falling or shaking), slow down and instead let the dog take only one step, reward for this step, and slowly add more steps over multiple training sessions. If you notice your dog is having a really hard time with this trick, it is best to stop training for it completely.

CONTINUED...

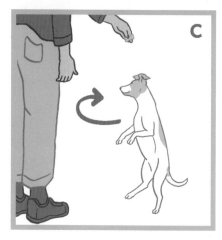

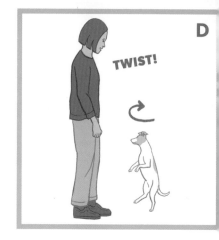

5. When the dog consistently follows your hand full circle, start adding a voice command every time your dog is about to spin around. You could use different commands for clockwise and counterclockwise turns (for example, "turn" and "twist"). **(Refer to example C.)**

6. During each training session, try to reduce your hand signal by moving your hand away from the dog. When the dog knows to turn around with the use of a voice command and a minimal hand cue or none at all, your dog has fully mastered the trick! **(Refer to example D.)**

AROUND YOU IN A CIRCLE (ORBIT)

Teach your dog to walk around you, backward and forward!

NOT SUITABLE FOR

- Dogs with joint issues, including hip dysplasia, spondylosis, and osteoarthritis.

COMMANDS/ TRICKS YOUR DOG SHOULD KNOW

- Stand

WHAT YOU NEED

- Treats
- Clicker

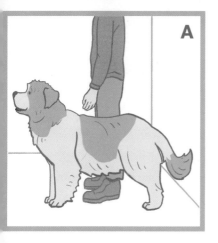

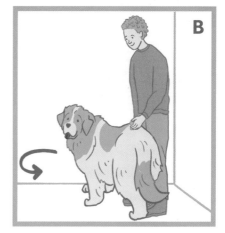

HOW TO TRAIN

1. Stand in the corner of a room, but with enough distance between the two walls that the dog can walk between you and the wall. Ask your dog to stand next to you on the left side. Hold treats in both of your hands. **(Refer to example A.)**

2. With your left hand, hold a treat in front of the dog's nose. Once they are interested in the treat, start to move your left hand away from your body to the left side of the dog's head, so you have to stretch out your arm and the dog has to look away from you in order to follow the treat.

3. **For a backward orbit (counter-clockwise):** Move your hand slowly toward the back of the dog (in a circular motion). In order to follow the treat, the dog will have to walk backward, and, because they are looking to one side, the dog will almost automatically walk toward the side they are facing away from (which will result in the dog making a circular motion around you). If the dog doesn't automatically stay close to you, the corner wall will help. Start by clicking and rewarding for only one step backward, and slowly add more steps. **(Refer to example B.)**

CONTINUED...

4. **For a forward orbit (clockwise):** Same as above, but moving your hand forward.

5. You will have to switch hands in order to be able to keep luring the dog all the way around you. Once the dog is standing behind you, switch hands behind your back, so that now you're luring the dog with your right hand (this is why it is important to keep treats in both hands). Continue step 2 with your right hand. **(Refer to example C.)**

6. Keep rewarding for one or two steps extra, until your dog has made a full circle around you. It may be tempting to start asking your dog for a full circle right away, but this will not work if the dog doesn't understand how to do this step-by-step first. In the end, small steps spread out over multiple short training sessions work faster and better!

7. After a couple of successful repetitions, add a voice command each time your dog starts to orbit backward (for example, "orbit" or "in" for counterclockwise and "out" for clockwise). Repeat the command every time the dog circles around you. **(Refer to example D.)**

8. When you're confident the dog understands the connection between the voice command and the trick, start to reduce the luring by slowly moving your hand away from the dog's nose and reducing the circular motion, until the dog will orbit on voice command only.

BACKWARD LEG WEAVE

Most people know the forward leg weave, but the backward leg weave is even more impressive.

NOT SUITABLE FOR

- Dogs with certain types of joint issues.

COMMANDS/TRICKS YOUR DOG SHOULD KNOW

- Stand
- Around You in a Circle (Orbit) (page 126) is useful but not necessary
- Walk Backward (page 44) is useful to know

WHAT YOU NEED

- Treats
- Clicker

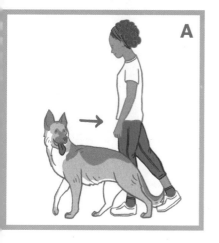 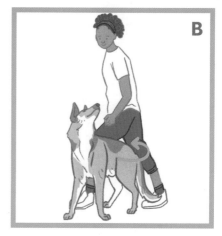

HOW TO TRAIN

1. Have the dog stand to your left. Hold treats in both of your hands. **(Refer to example A.)**

2. Take a big step backward with your right foot, to create a space large enough for your dog to walk through.

3. **If your dog already knows how to orbit on command (both ways):** Give the dog the command for orbit counterclockwise. It may help to lure the dog a little bit the first few times, so the dog understands it is okay to orbit around only one leg. Reward the dog when they are standing between your legs.

If your dog doesn't know orbit: Hold the treat in front of the dog's nose. Once they are interested in the treat, start moving your left hand away from your body to the left side of the dog's head, so you have to stretch out your arm and the dog has to look away from you in order to follow the treat. Then move your hand slowly toward the back of the dog in a circular motion. In order to follow the treat, the dog will have to walk backward, and, because they are looking to one side, they will almost automatically walk toward the side they are facing away from (which will result in the dog making a circular motion around your left leg). Start by clicking and rewarding for only one step backward, and slowly add more steps until the dog goes from standing next to you to standing between your legs. **(Refer to example B.)**

CONTINUED...

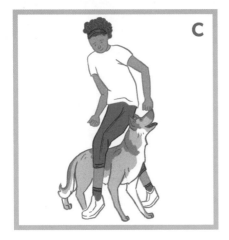

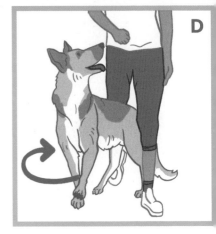

4. Once the dog is standing between your legs, ask them to walk backward until they are standing to your right. If the dog doesn't know this trick yet, hold a treat close to the dog's chest, so they will have to walk backward in order to reach it. Reward the dog well for walking backward. **(Refer to example C.)**

5. Take a big step backward with your left foot and repeat steps 3 and 4, now asking the dog to make a clockwise turn.

6. Repeat these steps, each time rewarding the dog well when they reach your other side. After several training sessions, add a voice command and reduce the hand luring. You can choose to give two separate commands for clockwise and counterclockwise turns (like you do for orbit), or one command for the entire backward leg weave trick. This comes down to a personal preference. **(Refer to example D.)**

7. When fully mastered, your dog should be able to weave backward between your legs with as minimal luring as possible.

DOG CATCH

With this trick, you will teach your dog to jump up into your arms.

NOT SUITABLE FOR

- Dogs too large to be caught so think about if it will be safe (both for you and the dog) to hold the weight of your dog before beginning training. Also, some dogs are not comfortable being held. If this is the case with your dog, you may want to skip this trick.

COMMANDS/TRICKS YOUR DOG SHOULD KNOW

- Jump into or on Any Object (page 54)

WHAT YOU NEED

- Treats or a toy
- Chair
- Some books, a barstool, and/or a table

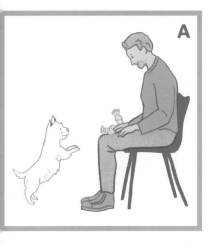

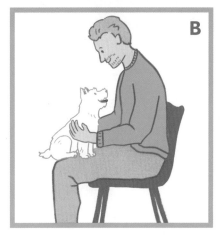

HOW TO TRAIN

1. To teach your dog to jump up toward you, it is best to start low, like while you are sitting on a chair. Place the chair in a room with a floor that provides plenty of grip (like a carpet). **(Refer to example A.)**

2. Sit in the chair, hold a reward in one hand, and encourage your dog to jump up. Praise and reward the dog when they jump up on your lap.

3. Repeat step 2 several times over the course of a few days, so the dog becomes comfortable with jumping up on your lap. Each time your dog is sitting on your lap, hold your arms around them for a few seconds so they get used to the feeling of you holding them. **(Refer to example B.)**

CONTINUED...

4. Now it is time to slowly increase the height your dog needs to jump. You could start by adding books to the seat of the chair, so you have to sit a bit higher, or you could use a barstool or, later on, a table. Make sure your feet are always on the ground, as, in the end, you will have to stand. Again, hold your arms around the dog immediately after they jump up. **(Refer to example C.)**

5. After multiple training sessions over several days, you should be able to stand up and have your dog jump up into your arms.

The easiest way to catch/hold your dog is to hold one arm under the dog's front legs and the other arm under the dog's butt (behind the dog's hind legs). This way, you're not holding the dog by their belly, which can be quite uncomfortable for them.

6. Keep repeating until your dog is fully comfortable with jumping into your arms. I only use a body cue as a command (calling my dog's name and spreading out my arms), but you could also use a voice command. Repeat the command each time your dog is about to jump up to you, so they learn the connection between jumping up and the command. **(Refer to example D.)**

REBOUND OFF A WALL

With the rebound trick, you will teach your dog to jump up to a wall, take off first with their front paws and then their hind paws, and then land on the ground.

NOT SUITABLE FOR

- Puppies or growing young dogs and dogs with obesity or joint issues. It is also not recommended for giant or heavy breeds, as their size and weight may make the trick physically difficult or even impossible to perform.

COMMANDS/TRICKS YOUR DOG SHOULD KNOW

- Jump into or on Any Object/Off (page 54)

WHAT YOU NEED

- A stable item (like a table) for the dog to jump up onto
- Treats or a toy
- A large board (one that is at least twice the size of the dog)

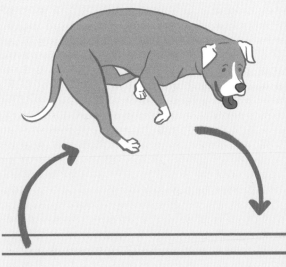

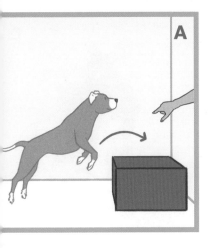

HOW TO TRAIN

1. Place an item, like a low table, next to a wall. Make sure both it and the floor provide plenty of grip so the dog doesn't slip when taking off or landing.

2. Have your dog jump up on the item. **(Refer to example A.)**

3. When the dog jumps up, immediately throw a treat or toy. Make sure you throw it in the opposite direction of where the dog came from. **(Refer to example B.)**

4. Repeat steps 2 and 3 several times, so your dog becomes comfortable with both jumping up and off the object quickly.

5. At this time, you can start to add a voice command (for example, "rebound") each time the dog jumps up onto the item.

CONTINUED...

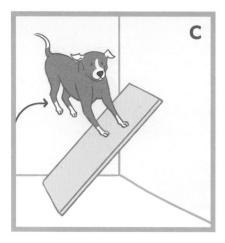

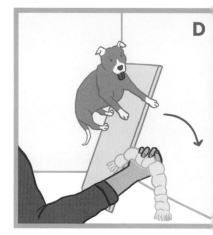

6. Now place a large board against the wall at a slight angle (it should still be relatively easy for your dog to jump up on the board). Make sure the board can't slip when the dog jumps up on it (you could, for example, place something heavy at the bottom of it to keep it from sliding). Repeat steps 2 and 3. **(Refer to example C.)**

7. Once the dog is comfortable with jumping onto and off the slanted board, stop throwing the treat or toy, but instead hold it in your hand and encourage the dog to catch it from your hand. This will automatically encourage the dog to jump higher, which will look more impressive. **(Refer to example D.)**

8. Once jumping up the slanted board goes well, you can start to increase the angle of the board (make sure you spread this out over multiple training sessions) until, finally, the board is standing vertically up against the wall.

9. Now remove the board and ask the dog to jump up against the wall instead. Reward and praise your dog enthusiastically when they do this.

10. Repeat step 9 until the dog is fully comfortable with doing a wall rebound.

11. Next you could try other objects like trees. Make sure the object you ask your dog to rebound against is always safe and non-slippery.

TAKE IT UP A NOTCH: You can also teach your dog to do a body rebound. The steps are similar to that of a wall rebound, but instead ask your dog to jump up and off your lap. Slowly increase the height like you did with Dog Catch (page 134), and encourage the dog to take off against your body by throwing a treat or toy every time the dog jumps up.

LIFT UP HIND LEG

This trick is especially fun to teach a female dog—I call it the "How Do Male Dogs Pee?" trick.

NOT SUITABLE FOR

- Puppies, as they haven't yet developed proper balance and hind leg awareness.

COMMANDS/TRICKS YOUR DOG SHOULD KNOW

- Stand

WHAT YOU NEED

- Treats
- Clicker

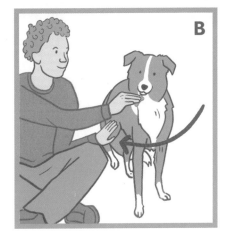

HOW TO TRAIN

1. Sit on the ground and have your dog stand next to you. **(Refer to example A.)**

2. Hold a treat in one hand, and hold this hand in front of the dog's nose. Hold the clicker in the other hand. With the clicker hand, start to stroke or apply pressure to the front of the dog's hind leg. This will make the dog lift up their leg (or, if this doesn't work, try to touch the bottom of that foot). Immediately click and reward when the dog lifts up the leg, even if it is just for a split second. **(Refer to example B.)**

3. Repeat step 2 over and over and over (over multiple training sessions), and try to slowly increase the time the leg is lifted up by waiting a bit longer with the click and reward. Most dogs find it very difficult to coordinate their hind legs, so it may take quite some

time. Be patient and keep training sessions short.

4. When the dog consistently lifts up the hind leg when you touch it, you can add a voice command (for example, "how do male dogs pee?") each time your dog lifts up their leg.

5. Once you have repeated these steps multiple times, you can start to minimize the touching, so the dog learns to lift up the leg on a voice command only. Try to have the dog lift up the leg when you gently tap it; stop tapping as soon as the dog lifts up the leg, then immediately click and reward.

6. Repeat step 5 and slowly try to reduce the number of taps and the amount of pressure you need to apply for each tap for the dog to lift up the leg. The trick is mastered when the dog lifts the leg on just a voice command.

WALK SIDEWAYS

While this may not be the first trick you think of to teach your dog, it does have some benefits, as it helps your dog raise body awareness and build strength, flexibility, and balance. Besides, it is pretty cool to see a dog mirroring their owner at a distance walking sideways.

COMMANDS/TRICKS YOUR DOG SHOULD KNOW

- Jump into or on Any Object (page 54) is very helpful

WHAT YOU NEED

- Book or low stool, something the dog can easily step onto with their front paws
- Treats
- Clicker
- Long bar or something else that is straight and slightly higher than ground level. The dog should be able to easily step onto it with their front paws.

HOW TO TRAIN

1. The first step is to teach the dog rear end awareness, something many dogs seem to lack. Lay a book (or set a low stool) on the ground and ask your dog to stand on it with both of their front paws. If your dog doesn't know how to do this, lure them toward the book or stool and click and reward whenever the dog touches it with one paw. When this goes well, keep luring until the dog places the second paw on it. Repeat this step until the dog is comfortable with placing both front paws on the book or stool.**(Refer to example A.)**

2. Have your dog stand on the book or stool with both front paws, and stand in front of the dog. Hold a treat in each hand, and keep them in front of you at the height of the dog's nose; make sure your dog is interested in the treats. Take a quarter of a step around the book or stool. Your feet should still be facing the book or stool. The dog should automatically follow by taking side steps around while keeping both paws on the book or stool. Finally, the dog should be standing right in front of you again. **(Refer to example B.)**

CONTINUED...

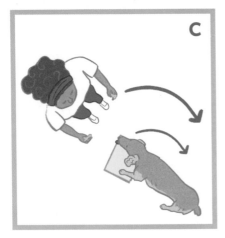

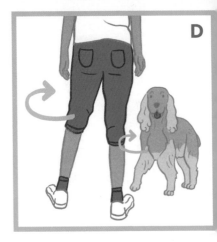

3. Repeat step 2, and slowly increase the number of steps until you can walk a full circle around the book or stool with the dog following you up on their hind legs. This may be difficult for the dog at first, so keep practicing in short training sessions. Once your dog masters going all the way around in one direction, repeat it in the other direction. **(Refer to example C.)**

4. Once step 3 has been mastered, you can repeat the sequence without the book or stool. Reward the dog well when they execute the desired behavior.

5. Now it is time to start working or walking sideways. Move your dog in a circle and then take one step to the side. Your dog should follow. Click and reward when the dog follows you and takes a step sideways. **(Refer to example D.)**

6. Slowly (step-by-step) increase the number of steps your dog has to take sideways. Make sure your dog's body is positioned straight in front of you when walking sideways. If your dog has trouble staying straight in front of you, this may indicate you are going too fast and need to slow down your pace.

   If your dog is not walking sideways like they should, you can lure the dog's head in the opposite direction that they need to walk to with a treat. This will cause the body to go sideways. Reward the dog well for this.

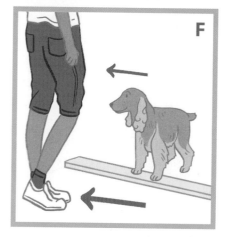

7. Repeat steps 5 and 6 until your dog can walk sideways in front of you for at least ten steps.

8. Add a voice command (for example, "side") each time your dog is walking sideways.

9. Lay a long wooden bar on the ground and ask your dog to step onto it with both front paws. Click and reward for this until your dog steps onto the bar without hesitation. **(Refer to example E.)**

10. Ask your dog to walk sideways (still in front of you) with both front paws on the bar. At first, this may be difficult for the dog, so start by rewarding for only one step and slowly increase the number of steps. **(Refer to example F.)**

11. Repeat step 10 until the dog performs the behavior correctly without any hesitation.

12. Now it is time to slowly increase the distance between you and the dog. Start with one small step backward and repeat step 10 every time you increase the distance a little bit. This may take quite some time, so be patient.

CONTINUED...

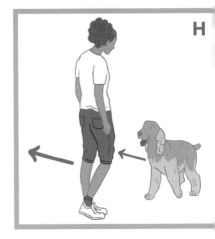

13. When you have reached a distance you like, instead of stopping with walking sideways when the dog has reached the end of the bar, ask for one or two extra steps sideways beyond the bar, so the dog learns to walk sideways at a distance without the bar guiding them. **(Refer to example G.)**

14. Repeat step 13. This can be quite difficult for a dog, so follow the dog's pace. Once the dog is comfortable with walking sideways at a distance without the bar being there as a guide, you can start practicing without the bar being there at all. **(Refer to example H.)**

15. Keep practicing until the dog can walk sideways at a distance on voice command and with your body cue (you walking sideways) only.

TEACH YOUR DOG CRAZY TRICKS

SKATEBOARD

This is probably one of the coolest tricks you can teach your dog, as well as being a fun way to exercise your dog.

NOT SUITABLE FOR

- Puppies or dogs with joint issues. The dog should be able to comfortably stand with all four feet on the skateboard and still have some space in front of and behind them, so this trick is not suitable for large or giant dogs.
- Skateboarding requires a lot of balance and strength from the dog; those who do not have this are at risk of falling. Keep a close eye on your dog, and don't ask them to do things they can't physically do. Teaching a dog to stand on a skateboard is relatively easy, but getting the dog to move the skateboard isn't. This is why some dogs may never learn this trick, even with lots of practice and training.

COMMANDS/TRICKS YOUR DOG SHOULD KNOW

- Jump into or on Any Object (page 54)

WHAT YOU NEED

- Skateboard
- Treats or a toy

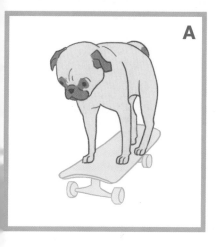

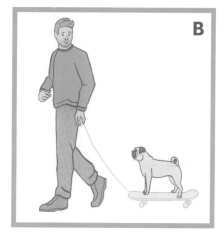

HOW TO TRAIN

1. The first step is to get the dog used to the skateboard without it moving. Tighten the wheels so they can't roll freely (there are special wheel straps that can be used for this). Place the skateboard on carpet or another type of soft flooring the board can't move easily on, and ask your dog to stand on it while you hold the skateboard still with one hand. Reward the dog when they stand on the skateboard. If your dog is hesitant, reward for one or two paws up on the skateboard first, until the dog is okay with standing on it with all four paws. Repeat this step until the dog is fully comfortable with being on the board. **(Refer to example A.)**

2. Release the wheels of the skateboard so it can move a little. Hold the skateboard still with one hand. Ask the dog to step on the board, have them stay on it for a few seconds, and then step off the board so the dog becomes comfortable with this move and builds muscle memory. Only move to the next step if you are sure the dog is comfortable with being on the board.

CONTINUED...

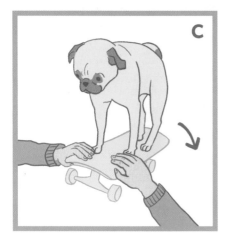

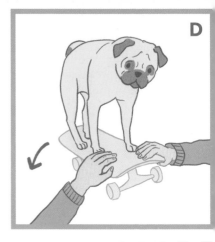

3. Now you can start to gently move (either by pushing it or by pulling it with a rope) the skateboard while the dog is standing on it. This can be done on a concrete floor or similar type of flooring that provides plenty of grip but makes it easier for the board to roll (make sure the environment is safe for the dog). Move it very slowly for a very short distance at first, to avoid your dog falling off and/or scaring them. Reward and praise the dog enthusiastically when they stay on the board while it moves. If the dog jumps off, ignore it and try again. **(Refer to example B.)**

4. Repeat step 3 over multiple training sessions, until the dog is completely comfortable with standing on a moving skateboard.

5. Now get your dog comfortable with the board moving from side to side. When your dog is standing on the board, gently rock it from left to right with your hand or foot. This will introduce your dog to this new aspect of movement and help build their balance. Keep doing this until the dog can hold their balance on the board easily. Keep training sessions for this step short, as balance training requires a lot of energy and asks a lot from the dog's muscles. If your dog starts to shake, it means you have been going on for too long and you need to stop. **(Refer to example C and D.)**

The reason for this step is that, to steer the board around, the dog will have to shift their weight from side to side by leaning to the left or right.

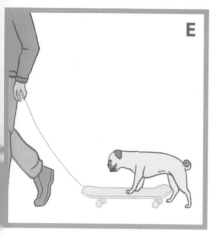

E

F

6. The next step is to teach the dog to push the board forward by themselves. Have your dog step on the board with only their front paws. Now move the board forward so the dog's hind legs have to "walk along." Keep a treat in front of the dog's nose to motivate them to walk forward. Reward and praise the dog enthusiatically for this. **(Refer to example E.)**

7. Repeat step 6, slowly minimizing your pulling or pushing until the dog is the one moving the board, pushing it forward with their hind legs (this may take quite a few training sessions to accomplish).

8. When the dog is able to move the board on their own, remove the rope if you are using one. Encourage the dog to move faster with the board and to jump up onto the board when it is at a speed, so the dog learns to only push the board to speed it up. **(Refer to example F.)**

9. Move to different environments and floorings so the dog becomes comfortable with skateboarding in different settings. Make sure the environment is always safe for the dog; dogs are smart, but, they don't know traffic laws!

CROSS PAWS (LYING DOWN)

Teach your dog to cross their paws when lying down.

NOT SUITABLE FOR

- Dogs with very short legs (like corgis and dachshunds) cannot physically perform this trick.

COMMANDS/TRICKS YOUR DOG SHOULD KNOW

- Give Paw (page 18), knowing both right and left paw
- Lie down

WHAT YOU NEED

- Treats
- Small table coaster or something similiar for your dog to touch with their paw
- Clicker
- Small piece of cardboard, sticky note, or anything else of a similar size that is flat

TEACH YOUR DOG CRAZY TRICKS

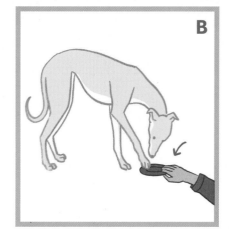

HOW TO TRAIN

1. Start by teaching the dog to touch a coaster with its paw. Hide a treat under the coaster and wait for the dog to scratch the coaster to get to the treat. Click immediately when the dog's paw touches the coaster and reward. Repeat this step several times. **(Refer to example A.)**

2. Hold the coaster in your hand, touch it to the ground, and wait for the dog to touch the coaster again. Click and reward. Repeat this step until the dog consistently touches the coaster with their paw when it is presented to the dog. **(Refer to example B.)**

   CONTINUED...

3. Present the coaster to the dog and ask for the right paw. Click and reward when the dog touches the coaster with the right paw and ignore when the dog touches the coaster with the left. Repeat this for both paws, switching up which paw you want the dog to touch the coaster with each time. **(Refer to example C.)**

4. Have the dog lie down, and repeat step 3 with the dog lying down.

5. Once your dog can execute step 4 consistently, you can work on having them cross their paws. With the dog lying down, hold the coaster to the left side of the dog's paws and have them touch the coaster with the right paw. Click, praise, and reward the dog well for this paw cross. **(Refer to example D.)**

6. For the left paw, hold the coaster next to the dog's right paw, in order to have the dog cross paws in the other direction.

E

F

7. Repeat steps 5 and 6, so the dog becomes comfortable with this move and builds muscle memory. Meanwhile, let go of the coaster so it lies flat on the ground, and, over time, move your hand away from the coaster.

8. If this goes well, exchange the coaster for something smaller, like a small piece of cardboard. Do this while you are practicing the trick with the coaster, so the dog isn't too aware of the switch. You may need to point out the piece of cardboard a few times, as the dog may be unsure what to do with it. Again, repeat this step until the dog is comfortable with the move.

9. Now remove the piece of cardboard and reward the dog well if they still cross paws. If the dog is unsure, point at the floor to see if that will encourage the dog to cross paws. If the dog doesn't cross paws, go back to step 8 and try an even smaller piece of cardboard before moving to step 9. **(Refer to example E.)**

10. Finally, add a voice command for each side (for example, "criss" and "cross"). You can also add a visual cue, like crossing your legs in front of the dog, so you and the dog cross your legs together. **(Refer to example F.)**

CROSS PAWS (WALKING)

While the first steps of teaching this trick are similar to those of teaching your dog to cross their paws while lying down, crossing paws while walking is a lot more difficult for the dog to do and will be more difficult for you to teach.

NOT SUITABLE FOR

- Dogs with very short legs (like corgis and dachshunds) cannot physically perform this trick.

COMMANDS/TRICKS YOUR DOG SHOULD KNOW

- Lie down
- Cross Paws (Lying Down) (page 154)
- Stand
- Give Paw (page 18), knowing both right and left paw

WHAT YOU NEED

- Two small table coasters or something similar for your dog to touch with their paw
- Treats
- Clicker
- Small pieces of cardboard, sticky notes, or anything else of a similiar size that is flat

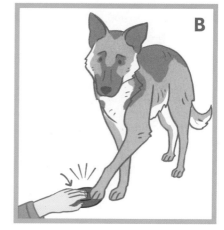

HOW TO TRAIN

1. Kneel on the floor and have the dog lie down in front of you. Have them perform the cross paws lying down trick a couple of times.

2. Ask your dog to stand up. Put a coaster on the floor and ask the dog to touch it with a paw. Click, reward, and praise the dog for doing so. Practice this step for both paws, using different commands for the left and right paw. If your dog is uncertain about touching the coaster, repeat steps 1 and 2 of cross paws lying down until they are reliably doing it. **(Refer to example A.)**

3. Repeat step 2 for both paws until your dog is clearly comfortable with touching the coaster while standing, as well as using the correct paw nearly every time you ask.

4. Now work on holding the position when the dog touches the coaster. The goal is for the dog to stand on the coaster until you give another command. Instead of clicking immediately when the dog touches the coaster, wait a second before clicking and rewarding. Slowly increase the time the dog has to stay in this position over the next few training sessions, until the dog can hold this position for around five seconds. **(Refer to example B.)**

5. Repeat step 4 for both front paws. When the dog is able to stay in position for around five seconds with each paw, you can move to the next step.

CONTINUED...

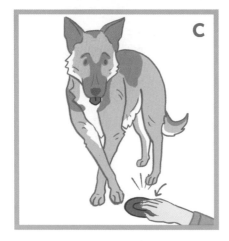

6. Now work on crossing the paws while standing. Put the coaster in front of the dog's left paw (make sure there is a little distance between the paw and the coaster) and ask your dog to touch it with their right paw. Click, reward, and praise the dog enthusiastically for this paw cross. Repeat this step until the dog consistently touches the coaster with the right paw and can stay in this position for several seconds. **(Refer to example C.)**

7. Now do the same thing for the left paw, placing the coaster in front of the dog's right paw.

8. Once the above steps go well, you can ask for a second step, where the dog crosses their paws. When the dog is standing with the right paw crossed to the left, place the second coaster immediately in front of where the right paw would have been if the dog hadn't crossed it. Now ask your dog to place their left paw on top of the second coaster. This results in your dog standing with their paws crossed. Repeat this a couple of times until the dog can perform this step every time you ask. **(Refer to example D.)**

This trick is quite difficult for dogs. If your dog moves the first paw away when having to take a step with the second paw, go back to step 6 and keep working on holding the crossed paw position for several seconds. Only reward the dog when they hold the position. If the dog moves, ignore it and try again.

9. Ask your dog to do the same thing but with the second step going the other way (stepping from the right side to the left side). Keep repeating this step, both ways, until the dog can perform these steps with ease.

10. Increase the time the dog has to hold their position by slowly increasing the time between the dog crossing paws and the click and reward, over multiple training sessions.

11. When this goes well, add more steps for the dog to walk with crossed paws like you did in steps 7 to 9.

12. Replace the coasters with small pieces of cardboard and repeat steps 7 to 9. Reward and praise the dog enthusiastically when they step on top of the cardboard pieces. Repeat until the dog crosses paws just as well with the cardboard as they did with the coasters.

13. The last step is to remove the cardboard pieces altogether. Repeat the trick a few times with the cardboard. Then stop placing new cardboard pieces in front of the dog, but still ask the dog to cross their paws. When they do, click, reward, and praise the dog enthusiastically. Repeat without having anything on the floor for the dog to touch. When this goes well, you have taught your dog to walk with crossed paws! **(Refer to example E and F.)**

If your dog doesn't want to cross paws without the piece of cardboard being there, try tearing the cardboard into even smaller pieces first and repeat the training before you remove them again.

WIPE YOUR FEET!

Help keep your house clean by teaching your dog to wipe their paws before entering!

WHAT YOU NEED

- Towel
- Treats or a toy
- Clicker
- Doormat

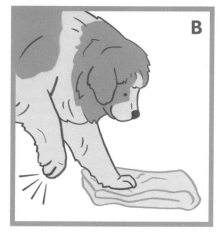

HOW TO TRAIN

FRONT PAWS

1. Place a towel on top of a door-mat. Scatter some treats or put a toy on it and fold the towel in half in such a way that the treats or toy is covered. (**Refer to example A.**)

2. Show the dog the towel and let them find the treats or toy. If the dog starts pawing at the towel, immediately click and reward the dog. (**Refer to example B.**)

3. Repeat steps 1 and 2 several times, until the dog starts to paw at the towel every time it is presented to the dog. Now you can add a voice command (for example, "wipe your feet!") each time your dog paws at the towel.

4. Ask the dog to "wipe your feet" without putting treats or a toy in the towel, and wait for them to start pawing at it with both front paws. Reward and praise the dog for doing this. Repeat this step several times, until the dog consistently "wipes" both front paws on command.

5. The next step is to have your dog wipe their paws on the doormat, without having the towel on it. Start out with the dog standing on the doormat with their front feet, and reward them for stay-ing on the doormat.

CONTINUED...

6. Ask the dog to "wipe your feet!" while standing on the doormat. Click, reward, and praise the dog enthusiastically when they start to do this. Repeat this step until the dog consistently "wipes" their front paws on command.

If the dog doesn't understand what you want, place the towel on top of the doormat and then give the voice command. Then take a smaller towel or fold the towel in half again to make it smaller. Repeat this step until the towel is as small as it can be folded. Then remove the towel and try to have the dog wipe their feet directly on the doormat again.

REAR PAWS

1. Teaching your dog to wipe their rear paws is a lot more difficult, so much so that there is a big chance that your dog will not learn this part of the trick. Some dogs will wipe their hind feet in the grass after doing their business. "Marking" this behavior with the clicker is key to teaching this part of the trick.

2. When your dog wipes their hind feet during a walk or after doing their business, click and immediately reward and praise your dog. Repeat this step every time your dog wipes their hind feet on their own. **(Refer to example C.)**

3. Once you've repeated step 1 a few times, add a voice command (for example, "wipe your hind feet!") each time your dog wipes their hind feet on their own.

4. Once you have repeated step 2 at least 15 times, try having the dog wipe their feet on command. The first few times, try to do this in a place your dog usually shows this behavior, and reward and praise the dog enthusiastically if they wipe their hind feet.

5. When step 4 goes well, start asking for the behavior in other places to see if they will still do it.

6. Only when the dog will wipe their feet every single time you ask them to should you move the dog to the doormat. If your dog already knows how to wipe their front feet, they may start with this. Wait until the dog also wipes their hind feet, then reward and praise the dog enthusiastically. **(Refer to example D.)**

7. Repeat until the dog consistently wipes all four feet on your command.

THE FLOOR IS LAVA

This is a children's game where everyone has to find an object to climb or jump up onto in order to get off the floor as fast as possible. The person who's last loses!

The basis of this trick is Jump into or on Any Object. However, now you want your dog to think for themselves and decide which object to jump on without receiving any kind of cue from you (no hand signals, voice command, pointing, nothing). This can be quite difficult, as your dog will have to figure out which objects can and can't be jumped up on by themselves.

NOT SUITABLE FOR

- Puppies and dogs with joint or obesity issues, as jumping on and off objects will put extra pressure on the joints. Otherwise, this trick is suitable for most dogs, as long as they are able to jump well.

COMMANDS/TRICKS YOUR DOG SHOULD KNOW

- Jump into or on Any Object (page 54)

WHAT YOU NEED

- Treats or a toy
- A field or area with plenty of safe objects that the dog can stand on (for example, a low table, chair, large rock, cushion, tree stump). Make sure the objects provide for plenty of grip so the dog won't slip and fall. Also make sure the surface underneath these objects provides plenty of grip, so the dog won't slip and fall while taking off or jumping down.

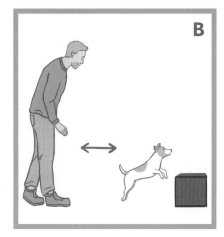

HOW TO TRAIN

1. Have the dog jump up on all of the objects in the area (using the command the dog already knows for this trick), so they learn that these objects are safe to stand on. Try to limit the use of hand signals from the start. **(Refer to example A.)**

2. Once that goes well, increase the distance between you and your dog step-by-step, rewarding the dog well for jumping up on an object every time. **(Refer to example B.)**

3. When the dog will jump up on an object from any distance on voice command only (no pointing at it), turn your back to the dog and ask them to jump up on the objects again, rewarding them well when they do.

Turning your back on your dog may confuse them, resulting in the dog trying to get in front of you instead of jumping up. Simply turn your back to the dog again and try again.

CONTINUED...

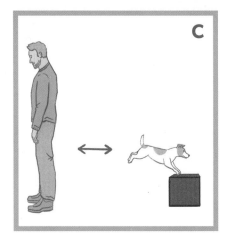

4. Repeat step 3 until your dog will consistently jump up on an object with your back facing them. **(Refer to example C.)**

5. Now it is time to add a new command, "the floor is lava," right after you give the dog the command to jump up on an object, followed by a reward and lots of praise.

6. Repeat step 5 until the dog responds by jumping up on an object when hearing just "the floor is lava."

7. Stand in the middle of an area that is filled with different objects for the dog to jump up on. Do not look at the dog or any specific object and only say "the floor is lava." Wait for the dog to jump up on an object. Praise the dog enthusiastically for doing so.

   If there is one specific object the dog keeps choosing to jump up on, remove this item so the dog will have to choose something else.

8. The last step is to have the dog jump up on an object while you do the same. Start by moving slowly. If it goes well, increase the speed. Reward and praise the dog enthusiastically when they move in a different direction than you and jump up on an object. **(Refer to example D.)**

EXPERT DOG TRICKS

Expert dog tricks are the hardest to teach your dog. These will either ask a lot from your dog in terms of strength and balance, or they are a combination of several different tricks in a row that together form a new behavior. Teaching these will require unending amounts of patience from you. And even with a lot of training, your dog may not be able to learn or perform some (or maybe all) of these; either your dog doesn't understand the trick or can't physically execute it. In such cases, continuing with training will only lead to stress, frustration, and possibly injury, so it is best (for the dog and your relationship with your dog) to stop. Never get mad at your dog for not being able to perform a trick.

BACKSTALL

Once your dog knows how to stand on an object, you can kick it up to have them stand on your back!

NOT SUITABLE FOR

- Puppies, growing young dogs, and dogs with joint or obesity issues, as they will have to jump off your back (this will put extra pressure on the joints). There is also the danger that the dog could fall off your back, resulting in injury. As the dog will have to stand on your back, the dog should not be bigger or heavier than you can comfortably carry.

COMMANDS/ TRICKS YOUR DOG SHOULD KNOW

- Jump into or on Any Object (page 54)

WHAT YOU NEED

- Low object for the dog to jump up on, like an ottoman
- Treats or a toy

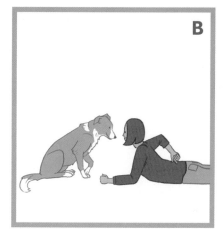

HOW TO TRAIN

1. To start, the dog must be able to jump up on an object while you lie down. To do this, ask your dog to jump up on an object multiple times while you are sitting or standing, then slowly change position so you are lying down. Keep rewarding the dog for jumping up on the object. When the dog will reliably perform the trick while you are lying down, you can move to the next step. **(Refer to example A.)**

2. Lie belly down on the ground. Let your dog sit to the side of you. With your hand on the other side, point at your back. While doing this, tell the dog to jump up. Reward the dog if they stand on your back. If the dog is hesitant, start by rewarding for two paws up first, and then slowly work to having all four paws standing on your back for the reward. **(Refer to example B.)**

CONTINUED...

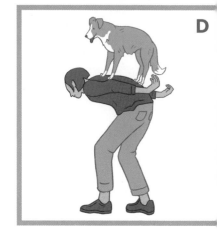

3. If the dog understands the trick while you are lying down, you can slowly start to move upward. The first step is to get on all fours, trying to keep your back flat enough so your dog can stand on it. **(Refer to example C.)**

4. Graduate so that you are kneeling down but not on all fours, with your back flattened enough so your dog can jump up. Once the dog will jump with you in this position, it is time to stand up. The final position will be you standing, bent forward, and the dog standing on your back! **(Refer to example D.)**

TAKE IT UP A NOTCH: To make this trick look extra awesome, have your dog Sit Pretty (page 86) on your back.

BALANCE SOMETHING ON NOSE

This trick will require lots of patience and calmness from both you and your dog.

NOT SUITABLE FOR

- Short-or snub-nosed breeds like French and English bulldogs.

COMMANDS/TRICKS YOUR DOG SHOULD KNOW

- Sit

WHAT YOU NEED

- Treats
- If you want, another object to balance

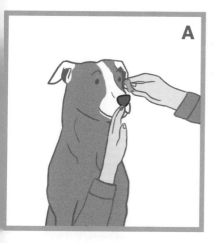

HOW TO TRAIN

1. Sit and ask your dog to sit in front of you.

2. Slowly place a treat on the flat part of the dog's nose. If your dog moves their nose while you try to attempt this, you can gently try to hold onto the nose with your other hand. **(Refer to example A.)**

3. When the treat is lying still on the dog's nose, immediately say "yes" or another word that indicates that the dog can drop the treat, then reward the dog. If you want, you can have your dog catch the treat directly off their nose. But you can also choose to remove the treat from the dog's nose yourself and give it to them by hand.

4. Repeat steps 1 to 3 over and over, each time slowly increasing the time the dog has to hold the treat on their nose, at the same time you also try to reduce having to hold your dog's nose still. Your goal is to have the dog balance the treat without your help. **(Refer to example B.)**

5. Start to introduce a voice command (for example, "wait") each time the dog is sitting with the treat on their nose.

TEACH YOUR DOG CRAZY TRICKS

HUG AND HOLD A STUFFED TOY

A dog hugging a stuffed toy with their front paws may be the cutest trick ever!

NOT SUITABLE FOR

- For dogs with joint issues because it requires a fair bit of strength and balance for the dog to both hold their position (sit pretty) and keep the stuffed toy between their paws. For these dogs, it is important to build up duration slowly and to keep training sessions short to increase the dog's strength and balance. This trick is not suitable for puppies. Dogs with short legs (like corgis and dachshunds) may not be able to physically perform this.

COMMANDS/TRICKS YOUR DOG SHOULD KNOW

- Sit
- Give Paw (page 18)
- Sit Pretty (page 86)
- The first steps (1 to 6) are similar to that of Hug (page 94)

WHAT YOU NEED

- Stuffed toy (like a teddy bear) whose length does not exceed the length of the dog's front legs and whose width does not exceed half the length of the dog's front legs
- Treats or a toy
- Clicker

HOW TO TRAIN

1. Sit and have your dog sit next to you.

2. Hold the stuffed toy in front of the dog with one hand, close to their chest in a horizontal position, and ask for a paw with the other hand. Instead of having your dog touch your hand with a paw, hold your hand close to the toy so the dog touches it instead. Click, reward, and praise the dog when they do this.
(Refer to example A.)

3. Repeat step 2 until the dog understands to touch the toy. The goal is to have the dog touch the toy with the inside of the paw. When this happens, click, reward, and praise the dog extra well. If your dog doesn't show this behavior on their own, wait a little longer with rewarding the dog for touching the toy. Most dogs will start to scratch the toy out of impatience, which will result in them touching it with the inside of the paw.
(Refer to example B.)

CONTINUED...

4. If step 3 goes well, ask your dog to sit pretty. When they do, place the toy between the dog's paws, close to their chest, and ask for a paw. When the dog touches the toy with the inside of the paw, click and reward the dog well. Start with rewarding for one paw, and if that goes well after several repetitions, wait for the second paw to touch the toy and reward for that. **(Refer to example C.)**

5. If the dog touches the toy with the inside of both paws, you can add a voice command (for example, "hug" or "both paws") each time your dog does it. Meanwhile, reduce the hand lure so the dog learns to hug on voice command only.

6. Now teach the dog to hold the position longer. Once the dog is touching the toy with both paws, very gently pull at the toy.

This will make most dogs hold onto it tighter, pulling it toward their chest.

7. If this happens and the dog is holding both paws tightly around the toy with it against their chest, let go of the toy for half a second. When the dog holds the position and doesn't drop the toy, click, reward, and praise the dog enthusiastically. Take the toy from the dog before they drop it on their own. **(Refer to example D.)**

Most dogs find it very difficult to stay in a sit pretty position, let alone to hold a toy between both paws while doing this. Keep training sessions very short to ensure you end each session before the dog gets tired or hurt. Don't get mad if the dog drops the toy, just try it again. If your dog has trouble holding the toy on their own, try again later and go back to repeating steps 6 and 7.

TEACH YOUR DOG CRAZY TRICKS

8. Keep repeating these steps. If everything goes well, you can slowly increase how long the dog holds the toy. Only increase the duration when the dog doesn't drop the toy (and can hold their position easily) at the current duration.

It may take several weeks to even months before the dog can perform this trick for several seconds in a row. Taking small steps is usually the fastest way to teach a dog this trick. So be patient!

HANDSTAND AGAINST A WALL

Teach your dog to stand with their hind feet against a wall, while still standing on the floor with both front paws.

NOT SUITABLE FOR

- Puppies, senior dogs, dogs with obesity or joint issues (like osteoarthritis, elbow dysplasia, or spondylosis, for example), dogs with short legs (like corgis and dachshunds), and most large and giant dog breeds (due to their size and weight). This is not a natural move for a dog and should be taught at a very slow pace. It will require a lot of strength and balance from your dog and it also puts significant pressure on the dog's joints. If you have any doubt about whether your dog should perform this trick, it may be better to not try it.

COMMANDS/TRICKS YOUR DOG SHOULD KNOW

- Walk Backward (page 44)

WHAT YOU NEED

- Objects that can serve as a platform, like books
- A wall (preferably textured, to provide grip) and flooring that also provides plenty of grip
- Treats
- Clicker

HOW TO TRAIN

1. Sit on the floor. Place a book on the floor right against a wall and position your dog in front of you with their back to the wall and the book. Make sure the dog isn't standing more than two steps (dog steps) away from the book. **(Refer to example A.)**

2. Tell the dog to walk backward. As soon as the dog places a hind paw on top of the book, click and reward the dog well.

3. Repeat step 2 until the dog consistently places at least one hind paw on top of the book. When the dog places both hind paws on the book, reward and praise the dog extra well. **(Refer to example B.)**

If the dog walks backward at an angle and misses the book, it might help to place a chair on either side of the dog so they are guided into walking backward in a straight line.

4. Once this step has been mastered, wait for the dog to place both hind paws on the book, ignoring when the dog only places one paw on the book. Most dogs will try to find a way to get the reward by starting to step around with both of their hind paws. Click, reward, and praise the dog immediately when they step on the book with the second paw.

5. Repeat until the dog consistently places both hind paws on the book.

CONTINUED...

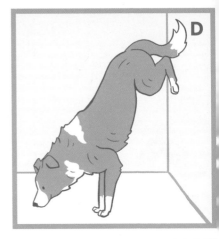

6. Now add a second book on top of the first one, so the dog has to step up a bit higher. When this goes well, you can slowly add more books to the pile. Do not add more than one or two books a week, as your dog needs time to build up their muscles (as well as muscle memory) in order to be able to perform the final handstand against the wall. Small steps are the way to go. Only add another book when the dog consistently steps onto the current pile without showing any signs of stiffness or stress. **(Refer to example C.)**

Once you have so many books that the pile becomes unstable, replace the books with sturdy boxes, storage containers, or something else that is stable and can hold the dog's weight.

7. When the pile becomes so high that the dog cannot reach the top of it with their hind legs, it is time to start practicing against the wall. Remove the pile and tell your dog to walk backward. If your dog places their hind paws against the wall, click, reward, and praise your dog extremely well. **(Refer to example D.)**

8. Repeat step 7 until the dog consistently places their hind paws against the wall (handstand against the wall). Work toward the dog placing the paws as high against the wall as they can. While practicing this step, add a voice command (for example, "handstand") each time the dog does a handstand against the wall.

TRAINING TIP: Keep training sessions short. Even when your dog knows this trick, do not ask them to perform it longer than a few minutes or more than three days a week.

9. When the dog understands the voice command for handstand and will perform this trick against the wall each time you ask, it is time to practice it against different walls in different locations. This way, your dog will become more confident with performing it.

CLEAN UP YOUR TOYS!

If you have a dog like mine, your floor is always full of toys! Teach your pup how to put them back where they belong!

COMMANDS/TRICKS YOUR DOG SHOULD KNOW

- Hold or Carry Something in the Mouth/Drop It (page 70)

WHAT YOU NEED

- Basket to serve as a toy box
- Toys
- Treats
- Clicker

HOW TO TRAIN

1. Place the basket in a spot where it will stay until your dog masters this trick, and put some toys around it. **(Refer to example A.)**

2. With one hand, point at a toy and tell the dog to take it. Hold a treat in the other hand and use this to guide the dog's head into the basket. Once the dog is holding their head in or above the basket, tell them to drop the toy. Once they drop it, click and reward the dog. **(Refer to example B.)**

3. Repeat step 2 several times, until your dog understands what you want from them. Switch up the toys you use every now and then, so your dog also learns that this trick doesn't apply to just one toy.

4. After several repetitions, add a voice command (for example, "clean up") each time the dog drops a toy into the basket. Reward and praise the dog well for this.

CONTINUED...

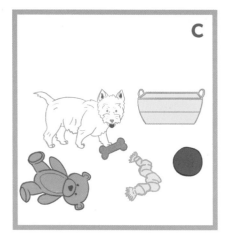

5. As your dog learns to drop the toys into the basket consistently, start to move the toys farther away from the basket. This way, the dog really has to walk the toy over to the basket, instead of just picking it up and dropping it almost straightaway. At the same time, reduce the number of times you give the dog a treat after a toy is put away, and instead ask for two and then more toys to be cleaned up for a treat. **(Refer to example C.)**

6. Over multiple training sessions, slowly move away from the toy basket, so the dog learns that they can still clean up the toys even when you aren't near the basket. Also slowly minimize or stop pointing out toys that need to be cleaned up and let the dog search for them on their own.

7. When the dog fully masters this trick, they should be able to clean up all their toys after hearing the command for "clean up" once. **(Refer to example D.)**

BURRITO ROLL

Teach your dog to roll themselves up in a blanket by grabbing one corner of it in their mouth and then rolling over.

COMMANDS/ TRICKS YOUR DOG SHOULD KNOW

- Lie down
- Hold or Carry Something in the Mouth/Drop It (page 70)
- Roll Over (page 40)

WHAT YOU NEED

- Blanket that is slightly bigger than the dog (if it's too small, you won't get a perfect burrito; if it is too big, the dog may have a problem rolling over with it)
- Treats

TEACH YOUR DOG CRAZY TRICKS

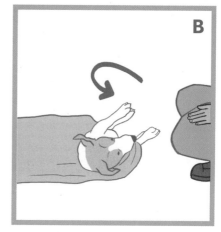

HOW TO TRAIN

1. Spread the blanket on the floor and have the dog lie down on one side of it (if the blanket has a short and a long end, have the dog lie down on the short end, facing the long end of the blanket). **(Refer to example A.)**

2. Have your dog grab the corner of the blanket that is closest to them. Repeat this a couple of times, so the dog gets used to lying down on the blanket and taking that corner of the blanket in their mouth. Make sure the dog doesn't stand up.

3. With the corner of the blanket in your dog's mouth, ask them to roll over. **(Refer to example B.)**

The goal is to have the dog roll over while holding the blanket. This may be confusing for the dog at first. Keep repeating this step, and encourage the dog to hold onto the blanket with your voice/tone (for example, by alternating the commands for "hold it" and "roll over"). If the dog rolls over a few times but doesn't hold the blanket while doing so, still give the dog a reward and stop training for that day. Try again another day.

CONTINUED...

4. Repeat steps 2 and 3 until the dog consistently lies down on the blanket, grabs the corner of it, and rolls over. Have your dog stay for a few seconds after rolling over, so you can get a good view of the "doggo burrito." Reward and praise your dog well each time.

5. Now add a voice command (for example, "burrito time"), saying it right before saying the commands on which the dog performs the sequence. Keep repeating this, and after multiple repetitions, stop saying the commands for the individual tricks. When the dog masters this trick, they should be able to complete the entire sequence after hearing the voice command for this trick only.

TEACH YOUR DOG CRAZY TRICKS

"LIMP" ON COMMAND

It's not fun when your dog has a limp. Unless...it's a trick!

NOT SUITABLE FOR

- Puppies, still-growing young dogs, and dogs with obesity or joint issues, specifically in the front paws, elbows, and/or shoulders (like elbow dysplasia). This may be extra hard to learn for heavier dog breeds and dogs with shorter legs.

COMMANDS/TRICKS YOUR DOG SHOULD KNOW

- Stand
- Give Paw (page 18)

WHAT YOU NEED

- Treats
- Clicker

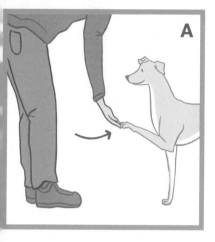

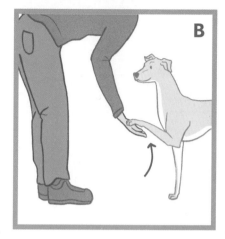

HOW TO TRAIN

1. Have your dog stand in front of you. Ask your dog to give a paw. Click, reward, and praise the dog for doing that. Repeat several times. **(Refer to example A.)**

2. Next, instead of taking the dog's paw immediately, wait half a second. Click, reward, and praise when they hold their paw in the air without placing it back on the ground again.

3. Repeat step 2, slowly increasing how long the dog has to keep their paw up in the air before getting a reward. Practice until your dog can keep their paw up for several seconds.

If your dog lowers the paw before you have clicked, gently tap at the underside of the dog's leg until they lift up the paw again. **(Refer to example B.)**

CONTINUED...

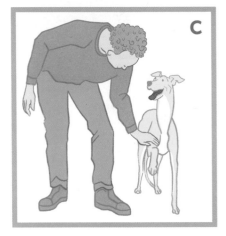

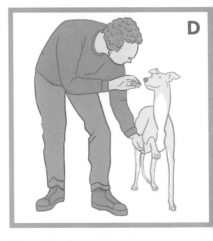

4. Now change your position. Stand next to your dog, preferably facing the same way as they are, and ask the dog to lift up a front paw. This may be confusing for the dog at first. If your dog has trouble with this, repeat steps 1 to 3 until the dog is comfortable lifting up a paw while standing beside you. **(Refer to example C.)**

5. Once the dog is able to lift up a paw and hold this position until you click, you can move to the next step: adding movement. Ask your dog to lift a paw. Hold a treat in front of your dog's nose with the hand that is the farthest away from the dog. Hold your other hand close to the leg that the dog needs to lift up, but don't touch it. Slowly move the treat in a straight line away from the dog. The goal here is to have your dog take a step while holding the paw up in the air. Most dogs, however, will place their paw back on the ground to take a step. If your dog lowers theirs, gently tap the underside of the paw to encourage them to keep it up. If your dog takes a step while holding the paw in the air, click, reward, and praise your dog enthusiastically. **(Refer to example D.)**

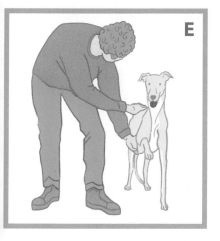

6. Keep repeating step 5. This trick requires quite a lot of balance from the dog, so do not rush training. It might take several weeks for your dog to master this step. If you have to help your dog by tapping the underside of the paw, slowly try to reduce the number of taps you have to give for the dog to keep the paw up, until your dog keeps it up while taking a step. Click, reward, and praise your dog well when they show the desired behavior. **(Refer to example E.)**

7. When your dog is reliably keeping the paw in the air as they take a step, add a voice command (for example, "limp") each time your dog takes a step with one paw in the air.

8. Once the dog is able to take a step on three legs without you tapping the leg, you can start adding more steps (one step at a time). Only increase the number of steps when the dog is able to take the current number of steps with one paw up in the air without any issues.

9. The last step is to remove the treat from your hand and reduce the luring over time. Reward your dog for walking with their paw up in the air on voice command, without any lure to motivate the dog to walk. **(Refer to example F.)**

FETCH A BEER FROM THE FRIDGE

How great would it be if your dog could grab you a nice cold one from the fridge while you're watching TV?

This is actually multiple different tricks that roll up into one trick. It is important that the dog has fully mastered all of these tricks before starting to teach them this one.

NOT SUITABLE FOR

- Puppies, as this trick is too complicated. Your dog needs to be motivated to perform tricks in order to learn and perform this whole sequence for you. Smaller dogs and toy dogs may have trouble opening a fridge door or carrying a beer can.

COMMANDS/TRICKS YOUR DOG SHOULD KNOW

- Hold or Carry Something in the Mouth/Drop It (page 70)
- Fetch and Retrieve an Object by Name (page 74)
- Close the Door (page 106)

WHAT YOU NEED

- Rope
- Fridge
- Treats
- Beer can

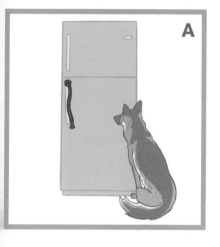

HOW TO TRAIN

1. Attach a rope to the fridge door handle. The rope should be long enough for your dog to easily reach it. **(Refer to example A.)**

2. Have your dog take the rope and tug it. You can motivate your dog to tug the rope by asking them to "bring it to you." Reward and praise the dog enthusiastically for pulling the rope. **(Refer to example B.)**

3. Repeat step 2 until the dog tugs the rope hard enough to open the door. Reward and praise your dog extra well when the door opens, so the dog knows that the door opening is what you want from them. **(Refer to example C.)**

4. Repeat step 3 several times so the dog becomes comfortable with this action.

CONTINUED...

5. Now teach your dog what a beer can is and to fetch it. Once your dog knows what a beer can is, place it in the fridge (on one of the bottom shelves or in the door, so the dog can easily reach it). Have your dog fetch the beer can from the fridge several times, so they become comfortable with this part of the trick. **(Refer to example D.)**

6. Once the dog knows these two tricks, you can combine them. Ask your dog to open the door, and, instead of rewarding for this, ask your dog to grab a beer from the fridge and bring it to you. When the dog has given the beer to you, then reward them. Keep repeating this step so your dog learns that these two behaviors are connected.

7. Meanwhile, work on a new voice command. Instead of having to give commands for opening the door, taking the beer, and bringing the beer, you want to give the dog a single command—"fetch me a beer." Give the command "fetch me a beer" while the dog is tugging the rope to open the fridge. Then, wait for your dog to grab a beer and bring it to you without saying anything at first. If your dog doesn't retrieve the beer, you can repeat the command "fetch me a beer." Reward and praise your dog extremely well when they bring the beer after hearing only one command. **(Refer to example E.)**

8. Repeat this until the dog consistently opens the fridge door and brings you a beer after only hearing one command.

9. The next step is to have your dog close the fridge door. Repeat this step several times, until the dog is comfortable with closing the fridge door on command.

10. Now ask your dog to fetch you a beer, and then, instead of rewarding, ask your dog to close the fridge door. Only once the dog has closed the door do you enthusiastically reward and praise the dog. (**Refer to example F.**)

11. Repeat step 10 over and over. When the dog consistently fetches a beer and closes the door, you can stop giving the command to close the door. Instead, wait for the dog to close the door on their own. It can help to show your dog the reward, but not give it to them, as this will motivate the dog to keep looking for something to do to earn the treat. Reward and praise your dog extra well when they close the door without you giving the command for it.

12. Keep repeating step 11 until the dog consistently opens the fridge door, grabs and brings you a beer, and closes the door, all after hearing a single command.

SKIP ROPE TOGETHER

This impressive and difficult trick isn't only for your dog, no. You will also have to do a workout! This trick is very difficult to perform, as you and your dog need to be exactly in sync, and both of you should be in good physical condition.

NOT SUITABLE FOR

- Puppies, young growing dogs, and dogs with obesity or joint problems. It also isn't recommended for large or giant dogs. Because this trick will cause a lot of pressure on the dog's joints, your dog should be in good body condition to do this.

COMMANDS/ TRICKS YOUR DOG SHOULD KNOW

- Stand

WHAT YOU NEED

- Treats or a toy
- A soft rope that is long enough for you and your dog to jump over and light enough to swing around

HOW TO TRAIN

1. The first thing you have to do is teach your dog to jump in the air on command. You can do this by holding a treat (or, even better, if your dog likes them, a toy) high in the air in front of you. Reward the dog well when they jump to catch the treat or toy. Make sure your dog doesn't jump into you. If that happens, push them back and don't give a reward. **(Refer to example A.)**

2. Repeat step 1 until the dog becomes comfortable at jumping.

3. Add a voice command (for example, "jump") each time the dog jumps.

4. After a while, you can remove the treat or toy and (over multiple training sessions) move your hand away until the dog will jump up on voice command only. **(Refer to example B.)**

CONTINUED...

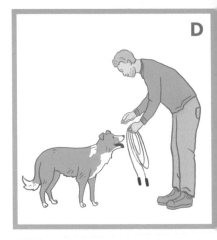

5. Next, teach your dog to jump up when you jump. Give the command to jump and, when your dog jumps, jump up yourself too. The first time you do this may be weird for the dog, so reward and praise them enthusiastically afterward. **(Refer to example C.)**

6. Repeat step 5 until the dog becomes comfortable with you jumping up with them.

7. After many repetitions, stop saying the command for jump and see if your dog will jump in the air when you do. If your dog jumps in the air with you, reward and praise the dog extra well. If your dog doesn't jump, keep repeating step 6 for a while and try again later.

8. Once your dog is reliably jumping up when you jump, you can introduce the rope. At the start, the rope may be scary for the dog. Have your dog stand in front of you, and hold a hand with treats in it in front of the dog's nose. With the other hand, slowly move the rope around the dog without it touching the dog. Reward the dog well for being accepting of the rope and for standing still. **(Refer to example D.)**

9. When your dog is okay with the rope, put away the treats and repeat step 8.

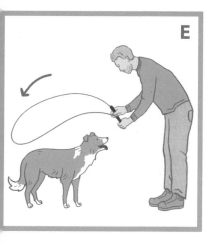

10. If that goes well, hold the rope in your hands like you would a jump rope. Have the rope lie behind you and gently swing it over you and the dog. Reward the dog well when they accept this and don't walk or scare away (if your dog does so, go back to repeating step 8). **(Refer to example E.)**

11. Repeat step 10 several times and, over time, slowly increase the speed of the swing. Make sure your dog is comfortable with this at all times.

If at any point your dog gets scared, go back to the previous steps. Your dog may need a longer introduction to the rope before you start swinging it over them at a speed. If your dog remains scared even after a proper introduction to the rope, it may be best to quit training for this trick.

12. Once the dog is fully comfortable with the rope swinging over both of you, you can start with the jumping. Swing the rope over both of you and, as you do this, jump up. Your dog should jump up as well. As you are both in the air, pull the rope under both of you so, when you land, the rope is behind you again (basically, the same as you would when skipping rope on your own, but now you do it with your dog). Reward and praise your dog enthusiastically for this. **(Refer to example F.)**

13. Keep repeating step 12. Start with just one jump, as this is difficult enough already. If this goes well, you can try to go for a second jump in another training session to see if both of you can pull that off. This may sound easier than it is, though!

ABOUT CIDER MILL PRESS BOOK PUBLISHERS

Good ideas ripen with time. From seed to harvest,
Cider Mill Press brings fine reading, information, and
entertainment together between the covers of its creatively
crafted books. Our Cider Mill bears fruit twice a year,
publishing a new crop of titles each spring and fall.

"WHERE GOOD BOOKS ARE READY FOR PRESS"

501 Nelson Place
Nashville, Tennessee 37214

cidermillpress.com